HIKING TRAILS

of

Northern Colorado

Dedicated to my hiking friends

Hiking Trails

of

Northern Colorado

By Mary Hagen

PRUETT **P** *PUBLISHING COMPANY*

Boulder, Colorado

Second Edition

3   4   5   6   7   8   9

Printed in the United States of America

Library of Congress Cataloging in Publication Data

Hagen, Mary.
    Hiking trails of northern Colorado.
    1. Hiking — Colorado — Guide-books. 2. Colorado — Description and travel — 1981–   — Guide-books.
I. Title.
GV199.42.C6H33 1985   917.88′043   85-3589
ISBN 0-87108-659-X (pbk.)

Contents

Foreword

The Big Thompson River and Cache La Poudre River rise high in the mountains of Rocky Mountain National Park. They cut their way through steep-walled canyons in their wanderings to the valleys of the High Plains. The many snow-capped peaks and gulches feeding the river systems are beauty spots accessible to the hiker.

The trails in this guide range from easy hikes to difficult hikes, but all of them can be made in one day. They extend from the Big Thompson River north to the North Fork of the Cache La Poudre River. Several of the trails are open all year, but during the winter months, weather conditions should be checked before starting out. Because of the elevation differences, the trails may be entirely forest hikes, tundra hikes, or a combination of forest and tundra. Some are cross-country treks. When no trail exists, walk carefully and do as little damage as possible to the fragile environment.

In a few instances trail accesses are being changed by the forest service. Those changes are mentioned in the text. If water is available along the trail it is, also, mentioned, but in a dry year the sources of water can dry up. Drink the water using your own judgement. Where the trails are difficult to follow because of marshes or meadows, they are usually marked by cairns, a pile of rocks, tree blazes, a long slash followed by a short in a tree about six feet above the ground, or a pole held up by rocks. These trail markers are usually placed so that when you stand next to one you can see the next.

In some instances trails in this guide wind into Rocky

Mountain National Park. If you plan to camp within the boundaries of the park you will need a permit. When hiking, be sure to sign in and out at the registers near the beginning of many of the trails to help the forest service and park service in the management of the trails.

Trail distances are based on mileages given by forest service signs or by measuring the trail on the map where no distances are given. Mileages to the trailheads by automobile vary according to the individual car odometer by as much as two miles. Therefore the distances given to the trailheads may differ from your readings. It is important to watch for highway markers in locating the trails. Hiking time is based on an average of two miles an hour. The *Roosevelt National Forest Map* put out by the U.S. Department of Agriculture, is an excellent map for locating trails mentioned in this guide. It is available from Roosevelt National Forest, Federal Building, Fort Collins, Colorado 80521, for a small fee.

Federal and state agencies are constantly upgrading and changing trails. Although every effort has been made to keep the trail information current, it is likely some modifications will have been made between reprint dates.

My special thanks go to Carol Bergerson and Mary Whitham who checked over the trails in this guide for accuracy, and who made most of the hikes with me. My husband, Harold, and Jackie Rounseville, also, receive my thanks for hiking with me and waiting patiently while I took notes and photographs.

Map Guide

Pingree Park Road and Poudre River Canyon (Middle)

68	Fish Creek	Pingree Park, Rustic
72	Little Beaver Creek	Pingree Park, Rustic
76	Dadd Gulch	Rustic
80	Mineral Springs Gulch	Rustic

Crown Point Road

86	Browns Lake	Comanche Peak, Kinikinik
90	Sheep Reservoir and Zimmerman Trail	Kinikinik

Pingree Park Road

93	North Signal Mountain	Pingree Park
96	Mummy Pass	Pingree Park, Comanche Peak
101	Emmaline and Cirque Lakes	Pingree Park, Comanche Peak
106	Stormy Peaks	Pingree Park

Upper Poudre River Canyon

109	Roaring Creek	Boston Peak, Kinikinik, Deadman, South Bald Mountain

Chambers Lake

112	Blue Lake	Chambers, Clark Peak
116	Twin Lakes	Chambers, Boston Peak

Tunnel Creek Campground

122	Branch Lakes	Clark Peak, Boston Peak, Rawah, Chambers
124	Twin Crater Lakes	Clark Peak, Boston Peak, Rawah, Chambers
128	Camp Lakes	Clark Peak, Boston Peak, Rawah, Chambers

Long Draw Reservior

132	Peterson Lake	Chambers, Boston Peak
134	Mirror Lake	Chambers, Comanche Peak

Colorado State Park

140	Montgomery Pass	Clark Peak
142	Snow and Agnes Lakes	Fall River Pass, Mt. Richthofen, Chambers, Clark Peak

Cache La Poudre River — North Fork

147	Middle and South Bald Mountains	South Bald Mountain
150	North Bald Mountain	South Bald Mountain

Addendum

155	Homestead Meadows	Panorama Peak
161	Comanche Lake	Comanche Peak
164	Comanche Peak	Comanche Peak
167	Browns Lake	Comanche Peak
171	Ruby Jewel Lake	Clark Peak
174	Lost Lake and Rawah Lake No. 1	Rawah Lakes

List of Trails

Destination	Distance	Elevation Gain	Trailhead

Big Thompson River and North Fork of Big Thompson River

Destination	Distance	Elevation Gain	Trailhead
Round Mountain	4.5 miles	2,690 feet	Loveland Mountain Park
Palisade Mountain	2.5 miles	2,114 feet	Drake, Colorado
Crosier Mountain	5.0 miles	2,850 feet	Devils Gulch Road
South Signal Mountain	5.0 miles	3,168 feet	Dunraven Glade
Crosier Mountain	4.5 miles	2,010 feet	Glen Haven

Lory State Park (Horsetooth Recreation Area)

Destination	Distance	Elevation Gain	Trailhead
Arthurs Rock	2.0 miles	1,180 feet	Lory State Park
Timber Trail	5.5 miles	1,260 feet	Lory State Park

Buckhorn

Destination	Distance	Elevation Gain	Trailhead
Sheep Creek and Moody Hill	5.5 miles	1,120 feet	Buckhorn Road
Lookout Mountain	3.0 miles	1,786 feet	Old Ballard Road
West White Pine Mountain	3.5 miles	2,017 feet	Buckhorn Road
Donner Pass to North Signal Mountain	7.0 miles	2,422 feet	Old Ballard Road

Poudre River Canyon (Lower)

Destination	Distance	Elevation Gain	Trailhead
Greyrock	3.0 miles	2,055 feet	Colorado 14
Hewelett Gulch	4.0 miles	640 feet	Colorado 14
Youngs Gulch	4.0 miles	1,160 feet	Colorado 14

Mount McConnel	2.5 miles	1,200 feet	Colorado 14
South Fork of the Poudre River	2.0 miles	903 feet	Colorado 14

Pingree Park Road and Poudre River Canyon (Middle)

Fish Creek	6.5 miles	1,040 feet	Jacks Gulch
Little Beaver Creek	3.5 miles	1,023 feet	Jacks Gulch
Dadd Gulch	3.0 miles	1,400 feet	Colorado 14
Mineral Springs Gulch	3.0 miles	1,935 feet	Colorado 14

Crown Point Road

Browns Lake	4.0 miles	780 feet	Crown Point Road
Sheep Creek Reservoir and	2.0 miles	760 feet	Crown Point Road
Zimmerman Trail	7.0 miles	1,880 feet	Crown Point Road and Colorado 14

Pingree Park Road

North Signal Mountain	7.0 miles	2,862 feet	Pingree Park Road
Mummy Pass	6.2 miles	2,480 feet	Tom Bennett Campground
Emmaline and Cirque Lakes	5.0 miles	2,063 feet	Tom Bennett Campground
Stormy Peaks	5.0 miles	3,120 feet	Pingree Park Road

Upper Poudre River Canyon

Roaring Creek	5.0 miles	2,300 feet	Colorado 14

Chambers Lake Area

Blue Lake	3.0 miles	1,320 feet	Colorado 14
Twin Lakes	4.0 miles	170 feet	Woods Landing Road

Tunnel Creek Campground

Branch Lakes	8.0 miles	2,444 feet	Woods Landing Road
Twin Crater Lakes	6.5 miles	2,403 feet	Woods Landing Road
Camp Lakes	7.5 miles	2,123 feet	Woods Landing Road

Long Draw Reservoir

Peterson Lake	10.0 miles	100 feet	Long Draw Reservoir Road
Mirror Lake	7.0 miles	1,200 feet	Long Draw Reservoir Road

Colorado State Park

Montgomery Pass	3.0 miles	1,000 feet	Colorado 14
Snow Lakes	5.0 miles	1,730 feet	Colorado 14
American Lakes	4.2 miles	1,410 feet	Colorado 14
Thunder Pass	5.0 miles	1,530 feet	Colorado 14

North Fork of the Cache La Poudre River

Middle and South Bald Mountains	6.0 miles	1,842 feet	Deadman Road
North Lone Pine Trail to North Bald Mountain	3.5 miles	1,582 feet	Deadman Road

Addendum

Homestead Meadows	4.0 miles	1,200 feet	U.S. Highway 36
Elkhorn Creek	4.5 miles	800 feet	Colorado 14
Comanche Lake	6.0 miles	560 feet	Comanche Reservoir
Comanche Peak	8.0 miles	3,622 feet	Comanche Reservoir
Browns Lake	7.0 miles	1,440 feet	Comanche Reservoir
Ruby Jewel Lake	1.5 miles	1,200 feet	Clark Peak
Lost Lake and Rawah Lake No. 1	10.0 miles	2,160 feet	Rawah Lakes

Big Thompson River and North Fork of Big Thompson River

Round Mountain

In Colorado, there are trails for all seasons. It is one of many reasons why Colorado has gained the reputation as America's truly outdoor state. While hikers in other states must patiently wait for their favorite trails to open and dry out from snow or rain, Colorado hikers select trails from one of several micro-climates. Hikers enjoy pleasant weather and superb scenic trails twelve months of the year.

One such trail ideal for fall, winter, and spring hiking is the Round Mountain Trail in the Big Thompson Canyon. The trail heads across the road from Loveland Mountain Park 3.5 miles east of Drake, Colorado on U.S. 34.

It is not a trail for the novice hiker, for it is a steep, long 4.5 miles to the end. The trail begins an immediate steady climb up the side of the mountain. Much of the trail is marked with attractive displays about the flora and fauna seen along the way. Once the trail leaves the river channel, it is a quiet hike through ponderosa pine, some aspen, and a ground cover of sage, mountain mahogany, kinnikinic, and, in the spring of the year, a different display of wildflowers every week.

After climbing steadily for about two miles, the trail levels out and cuts through granitic rocks. On either side of the trail are needle-like pinnacles. A miniature montane habitat of aspen, huckleberry, wild geranium, thimble-berry, and golden banner grow in a damp depression between the steep sides of the weathered rocks. The trail

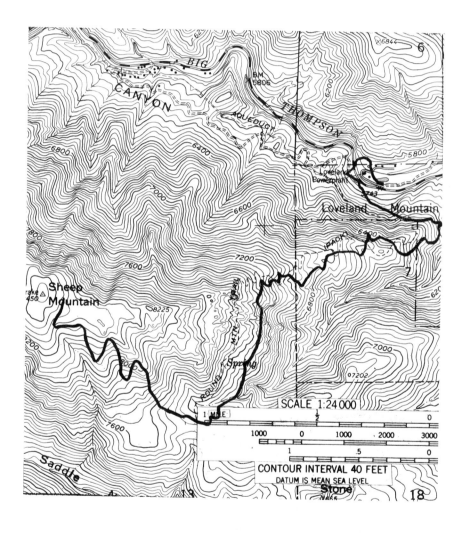

SCALE 1:24 000

| 1 MILE | | ½ | | 0 |

| 1000 | 0 | 1000 | 2000 | 3000 |

| 1 | | .5 | | 0 |

CONTOUR INTERVAL 40 FEET
DATUM IS MEAN SEA LEVEL

Rock cut on Round Mountain Trail

follows along the sides of the rock carvings, dropping gradually and leveling out. A small spring trickles from a stand pipe not far from the needles. The trail continues to lose elevation until it crosses a draw. From here to the end of the trail there is a steep climb through sparsely growing ponderosa pine. The trail is well marked with rock cairns and goes uphill to the northwest.

At the Summit, snow-capped peaks to the west are framed between the pines. The plains stretch endlessly to the east. At the foot of the mountain are Pinewood Lake, Flatiron Reservoir, and Carter Lake Reservoir.

Granite outcroppings above Round Mountain Trail

Trail through rocks on Round Mountain Trail

There is an elevation gain of 2,690 feet. No drinking water is available along the trail. Allow 3½ to 4 hours to make the hike one way.

For those who want something less strenuous than the Round Mountain Trail, there is a one-mile nature walk that heads in the same place. The trail is an old road that follows the Big Thompson River for one mile to an overlook. A rock shelter with a fireplace offers a nice place for a picnic.

Palisade Mountain

The hike from Drake, Colorado, on U.S. 34, to Palisade Mountain is short but strenuous. There are several geological zones that make this hike interesting. To begin the hike, park near the bridge over the North Fork of the Big Thompson River in Drake and walk along the northeast bank of the North Fork. After passing below the cabins, cut uphill to intercept a crisscross of horse trails. Continue hiking north up a steep, open hillside above Drake.

Along the way, watch for black chunks of tourmaline, a semiprecious stone, that is embedded in quartz. Here and there along the trail are intrusions of pegmatite in schist. Most of the rock on the climb to a small saddle is metamorphic.

When you reach the saddle keep to the right and continue uphill through a sparse stand of ponderosa pine. Climb past a pink outcropping of rock to a viewpoint of the Big Thompson River and Drake. Some juniper grows next to the trail. Crosier Mountain to the west is framed by the trees. Continue uphill in a northern direction along an obvious trail through an open park and past some metamorphic rock pillars until you reach a road. Follow the road to the right around a bend and to a vista of Pallisade Mountain. When the road bends sharply to the left (northwest) and begins to drop into a park, leave the road by turning right and begin working cross-country around the

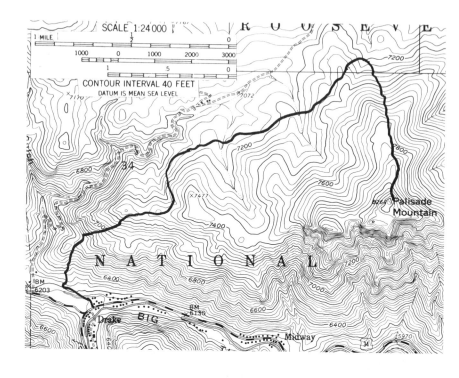

lower of the two summits of Palisade Mountain heading in a northeastern direction. Cross over a section of an abandoned fence to a drop downhill that goes north and slightly west. Angle east away from the fence.

A large ravine with a stand of dead trees must be crossed by staying high and hiking through the trees. After crossing the ravine, drop through a stand of aspen and head northeast uphill. Although the mountain is to the southeast, keep bending north toward a long ridge that leads to the summit. The last 100 feet of the hike is a scramble over huge slabs of tonalite and a climb through a small chimney. The high point of the 8,264-foot mountain is marked by wooden poles.

The view to the northwest from the mountain is somewhat obscured by trees. A scramble to a lower point opens up a fantastic vista of the mountains in Rocky Mountain

Summit of Palisade Mountain

Park. Because there is a 2,114-foot elevation gain in less than three miles, allow two to three hours to climb to the summit. Carry water.

Crosier Mountain

It is a steep climb of 2,850 feet in 5.0 miles to Crosier Mountain which is located in Roosevelt National Forest. The elevation of the mountain is 9,250 feet. From the summit, the hiker has an unsurpassed view of the eastern slope of Rocky Mountain National Park. The trail to the mountain is open most of the year, making it a good fall, winter, or spring trek. However, during the winter months, the weather should be checked before making the hike.

There are three accesses to the mountain. The first is a 2.2 mile drive on the Glen Haven road from its junction with U.S. 34 at Drake. Look for a small metal gate located on the

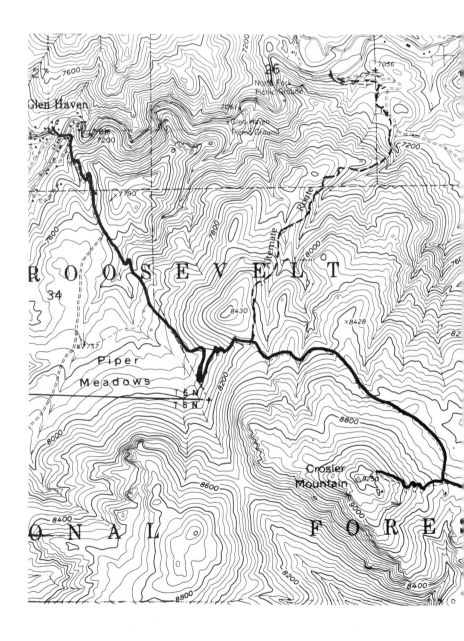

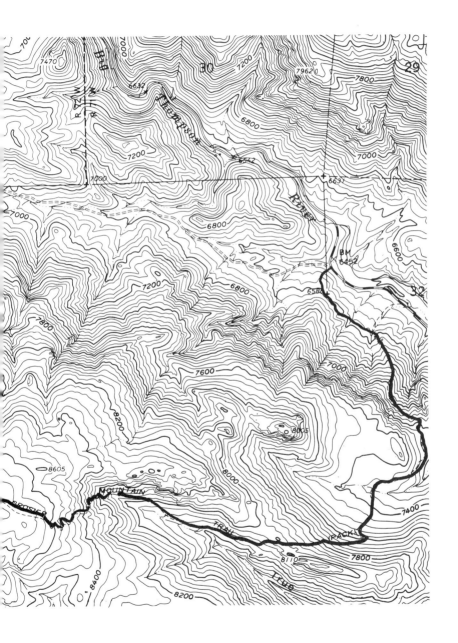

Meadow and unnamed peak on the way to Crosier Mountain

lefthand side of the road. Limited parking is available near the gate.

Pass through the gate and begin an immediate climb following the edge of a draw. The trail is faint but once you enter the trees, it is easy to follow. Continue uphill following the draw to its head making two switchbacks along the way. At the head of the draw the trail circles left past an abandoned mine. The trail winds uphill past a trail junction. Keep left at the junction and reach a small ridge. Walk through a fence. The trail bends beneath the base of a cliff and uphill over three switchbacks to a second ridge. For a short distance the trail is level.

The trail resumes an uphill grade to a meadow and disappears. Cut through the center of the meadow heading in a western direction and watch for a pile of rocks that at one time held a pole marker. Keep slightly left of center and work toward the trees. The trail can be picked up below and to the southwest of a pyramid-like granite peak. There are the remains of a fireplace built against the rock cliff near the trail. Once the trail is picked up, it winds alongside a small draw and to a crossing over the draw.

Continue uphill to a bend in the trail and turn west. Climb to a small notch in the rocks and the top of another ridge. After walking through a fence turn right and drop downhill to True Gulch. Gradually the trail levels and cuts through a large stand of aspen. At the end of the aspen grove the trail winds uphill and around a ridge. At the crest of the ridge Crosier Mountain comes into view through the trees. Walk along the trail to the Crosier Mountain trail sign. Take a left turn heading west and follow the unimproved trail to the summit for .5 mile.

No water is available along the trail. Allow two to three hours one way to reach the summit.

Unnamed peak on the way to Crosier Mountain

South Signal Mountain

It is a steep five-mile hike along Bulwark Ridge to South Signal Mountain located on the northeast border of Rocky Mountain National Park. To reach the trailhead drive to Drake, and turn onto the Glen Haven Road. Drive about 6.1 miles to a bridge on the right side of the main road that crosses the North Fork of the Big Thompson at the forest access sign. Turn and cross the bridge onto the Dunraven Glade Road. Continue over the unimproved road 2.5 miles to a parking area and hike .25 mile to the trail head on the right side of the road near a private gate.

The elevation gain is 3,168 feet from the beginning of the hike at the end of the Dunraven Glade Road to the summit. The trail climbs steeply to the north for about a mile and then branches left at the Miller Fork Junction, and climbs

Signal Mountains from Bulwark Ridge

South Signal Mountain

steeply for about three miles up the ridge through an evergreen forest. Although the trail is dry, many rare flowers grow in the moist areas under the pine and spruce forest, such as the beautiful lavender-colored fairy slipper.

Here and there along the trail, Longs Peak and Twin Sisters can be seen. The Signal Mountains do not come into view for the first three miles of the hike. Just below South Signal Mountain, a trail junction is reached. The left branch leads into Rocky Mountain National Park. Take the right branch to climb to South Signal Mountain and follow around the base of the Mountain below some cliffs and past a rock sentinel on the right of the trail. Come to a saddle between North and South Signal Mountain. Take off to the west and climb cross-country over the tundra to South Signal Mountain. The summit is marked with a cairn. The Signal Mountains are at the edge of the Mummy Range. From the summit, Stormy Peaks and the mountains above Lost Lake can be seen. It is easy to pick out the deep canyon

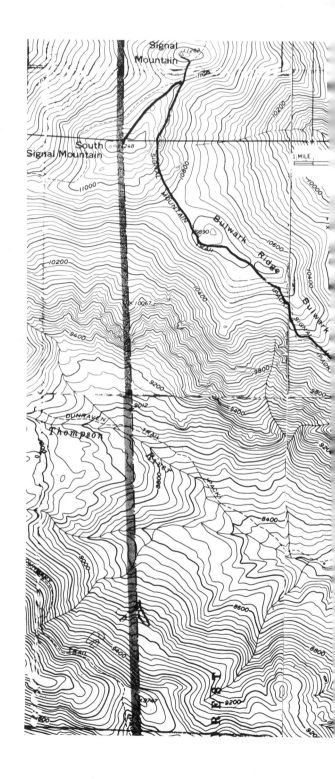

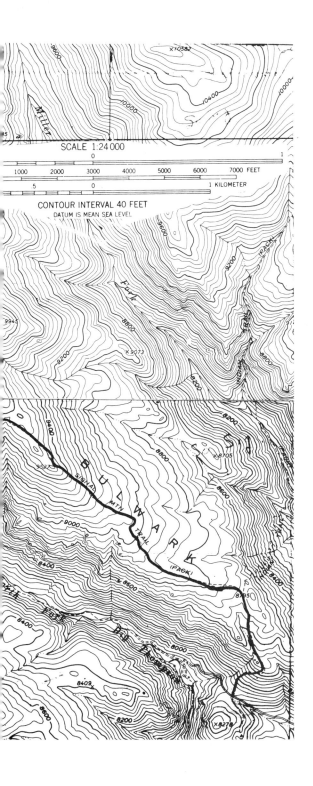

SCALE 1:24 000

CONTOUR INTERVAL 40 FEET
DATUM IS MEAN SEA LEVEL

Trail to South Signal Mountain

Crossing the tundra to South Signal Mountain

of the North Fork of the Big Thompson River. North Signal Mountain is within easy hiking distance by backtracking to the saddle and climbing to the summit.

If you wish, you can follow the trail around North Signal Mountain and come out on the Pingree Park Road. This adds seven miles to the trip and is written up in another section of this book.

No water is available along the Bulwark Ridge Trail nor on the Signal Mountains. Because of the steepness of the trail, allow about four hours to climb to the summit of the mountain.

An Alternative Route To Crosier Mountain

A second route to the 9,250-foot Crosier Mountain starts at Glen Haven. It is possible to make a round trip and come out on the Devil's Gulch Road. From Glen Haven, it is four and one-half miles to the summit, with an elevation gain of 2,010 feet. This compares to the 5.0 mile hike from the Drake trailhead with an elevation gain of 2,850 feet.

To reach the trailhead, drive through Glen Haven to the Livery Stable and park along the side of the road. Walk along the dirt road that cuts in back of the stable to the trail sign on the right side of the road. The trail makes an immediate series of switchbacks through an evergreen forest to a Forest Service sign that points to Crosier Mountain. Follow the trail over a gully and up several long switchbacks. Keep to the left as you work uphill. Crosier Mountain and an unnamed mountain will come into view.

When Piper Meadow is reached, take the left branch in the trail and cut along the east edge of the meadow. Work in a southerly direction to the end of the meadow and another sign. The Signal Mountains and Lumpy Ridge can be seen across the meadow. At the end of the meadow, turn left at the sign and work up a draw, making a series of

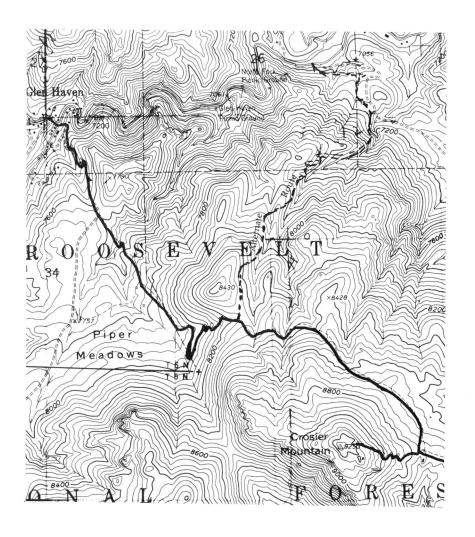

Crosier Mountain Trail from Glen Haven

Glen Haven Trail

switchbacks to a small saddle. You will come to a trail branch that leads back to the North Fork of the Big Thompson if you hike to the left or to Crosier Mountain if you bear straight ahead.* Continue by circling below an 8,430-foot ridge.

The trail meanders in and out of lodgepole pine, aspen, large conifer trees, open spots, and rock outcroppings. Reach a half-mile sign to Crosier Mountain and head west for a climb through the forest to the peak. Trees cover all but the small exposed granite cap that is the high point on the mountain. Carry water, because none is available along the way.

*This trail is the third access to Crosier Mountain. It heads 5.8 miles from Drake on the Glen Haven Road near a huge gravel cut. There is a locked metal Forest Service gate to keep livestock from drifting onto the highway that must be crossed. The trail is steep. It switchbacks for two miles to the saddle junction that comes from Glen Haven. On the route there are nice views of the Big Thompson Canyon and Pallisade Mountain. At one point near the saddle the trail branches. The left branch leads to Cougar Rock. It is a short walk with a nice view at the end.

Horsetooth Recreation Area

Arthurs Rock

Arthurs Rock is a Fort Collins landmark located west of Horsetooth Reservoir. Reaching it is a short, pleasant hike that can be made in a half-day. To reach the trailhead, drive to Bellvue and turn left or south at the Bellvue Post Office. Proceed for 5.4 miles to the Lory State Park which has an entry fee. The trail begins at the end of the road in the Park near the large sign showing a map of the area. It is 2.0 miles to the summit with an elevation gain of 1,180 feet.

Arthurs Rock Trail

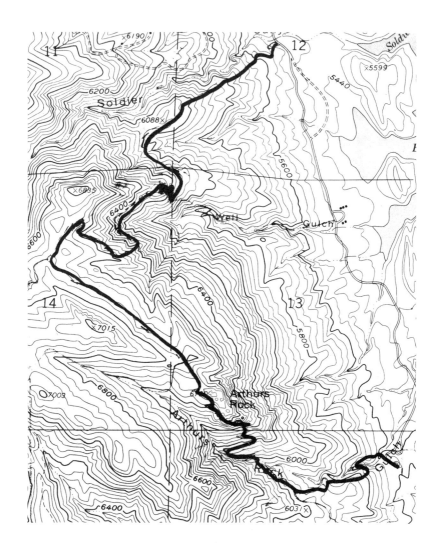

Arthurs Rock Trail

Woodland Nature Trail to Arthurs Rock

Cross a small bridge, followed by several steps and a series of switchbacks through a rock canyon. Cottonwood, chokecherry, willow, and ponderosa pine grow on the hills and in the canyon next to a small, intermittent stream. The trail winds uphill to the base of a rock cliff. After rounding the cliff and making a series of switchbacks, reach a saddle and a trail branch. To climb the Rock, go right, working your way around the base of the mountain to an obvious cut that leads to the summit of the 6,750-foot mountain.

The area in and around Fort Collins below resembles a huge relief map. Claymore Lake, Horsetooth Reservoir, and Fort Collins break away to the east. Once Arthurs Rock is reached, it is possible to branch out in several directions and explore the numerous rock outcroppings in the area. Carry water. None is available along the trail.

Timber Trail
To Arthurs Rock

Timber Trail heads at the first picnic ground inside Lory State Park 3.4 miles from Bellvue, Colorado. There is an entry fee to the park. To reach Bellvue drive to Vern's Place northwest of LaPorte on U.S. 287. Turn left off U.S. 287 at the Rist Canyon Road and drive to Bellvue. In Bellvue turn left or south at the Bellvue Post Office and continue to Lory State Park. Arthurs Rock is 5.5 miles with 1,270 feet elevation gain.

The first part of the hike is over a grass-covered hillside that has patches of mahogony and oak. There are a number of switchbacks that follow a canyon located to the north of the trail. Deer tracks crisscross the trail, and deer often can be seen grazing on the hillsides.

Gradually the trail bends around a knoll and to the head of a small canyon that is crossed. The trail parallels the knoll to a trail junction with Wells Gulch which comes in from the south. From the Wells Gulch junction, it is 2.2 miles back to the road or another three miles to Arthurs Rock.

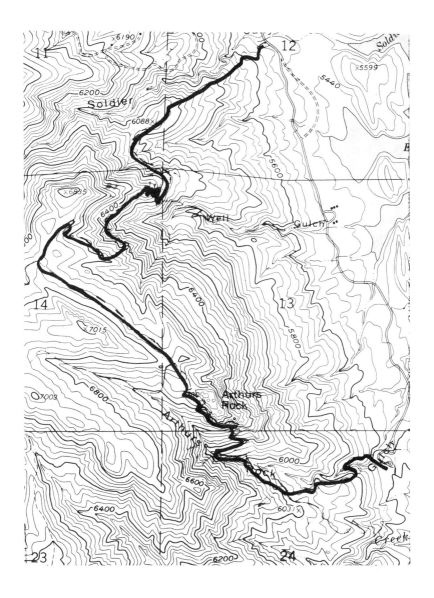

Timber Trail

Arthurs Rock from Timber Trail

To reach Arthurs Rock, keep right and climb uphill six switchbacks through an evergreen forest of Rocky Mountain juniper, Douglas fir, and pine.

Gradually the trail winds away from Wells Gulch to an overlook of Horsetooth Reservoir, Fort Collins, and the prairie. Above the trail is a granite outcropping. The trail levels and meanders through the forest to a trail junction. Take the left branch to reach Arthurs Rock. From the junction, it is one mile to the summit of Arthurs Rock over a fading jeep trail.

For a time the trail wanders up and down in an erratic pattern through the pine. Come to Woodland Nature Trail junction and turn left or north for a quick climb to the summit of the granite rock.

The Woodland Nature Trail drops downhill to a parking area that is two miles from the beginning of Timber Trail. Making a circle hike involves a walk along the road back to the Timber Trail parking area.

No water is available along the trail. There is an elevation gain of 1,260 feet.

Buckhorn

Sheep Creek
and
Moody Hill

An excellent spring and fall hike is over an old logging road to Sheep Creek. Along the way, herds of elk and deer are often encountered. The trail wanders over Moody Hill. There are several nice vistas of Boiler Hill and Crystal Mountain from the road. To reach the trailhead, drive to Stove Prairie from Bellvue. Turn left and continue 3.7 miles to the Buckhorn intersection, then turn right (west). Drive 1.4 miles to Sheep Creek. The trail heads at the stream and immediately bends west. It winds through a stand of ponderosa pine that has a population of Abert squirrels along the lower sections. The first part of the hike is steep. To the left can be seen the deep Sheep Creek Canyon.

Near the summit of Moody Hill, Crystal Mountain comes into view, and then Lookout Mountain can be seen. At the crest of Moody Hill, take a left at the first road junction and then a right at the minor junction. Several roads come into the Moody Hill and Sheep Creek Trail along the way. By following the main road, drop down to a major road, and, to avoid private property, cross this road. Climb through a pine forest and drop downhill to the Crystal Mountain Road. Continue straight ahead for a climb through pine, aspen, and around the edge of a meadow. Keep right at the next road junction. Go by the remains of an old log cabin,

Lookout Mountain

an intermittent spring, and a small mine. A short distance after the mine, there is a bend in the road. Still another road is encountered. The two join and drop downhill through a small meadow to Sheep Creek.

There is an elevation gain of 1,120 feet in about 5.5 miles to Sheep Creek. From Sheep Creek, there is a road to the west that leads away from Sheep Creek to Crystal Mountain. It involves another 1,146-foot elevation gain in 1.5 miles. The road ends at a mine below the mountain that is on private property. The summit of Crystal is not. No drinking water is available along the trail.

Note: This trail may later be designated as a National Jeep Trail.

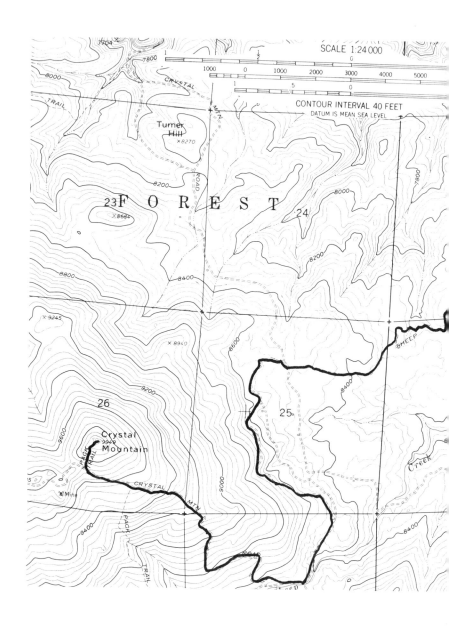

SCALE 1:24 000

CONTOUR INTERVAL 40 FEET
DATUM IS MEAN SEA LEVEL

Turner
Hill
×8270

₂₃F O R E S T   24

×8684

×9245

×8940

26

Crystal
Mountain
9949

25

Mine

CRYSTAL

SHEEP

Creek

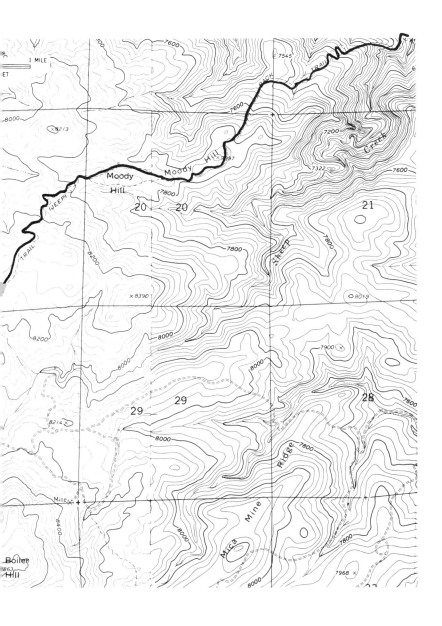

Lookout Mountain

From the 10,626-foot crown of Lookout Mountain, Longs Peak, Hallett Peak, Flattop Mountain, Lake Estes, and Estes Park can be seen in one direction. To the north, West White Pine Mountain and East White Pine Mountain are in view, as well as the Buckhorn Road and Buckhorn Ranger Station. Far to the east are the Great Plains. Stormy Peaks are to the west, and the Mummy Range is in view in the distance.

To reach Lookout Mountain, drive to Stove Prairie by way of Rist Canyon Road and turn left. Continue to the Buckhorn intersection and turn right for 10.6 miles to the Old Ballard Road junction. Drive left onto the Ballard road for 3.5 miles to the Donner Trail access. The sign is on the right side of the road. The trail access is on the left. No good parking is available at the trailhead, but the Forest Service is planning to build a parking area in the future.

From the trail to Lookout Mountain

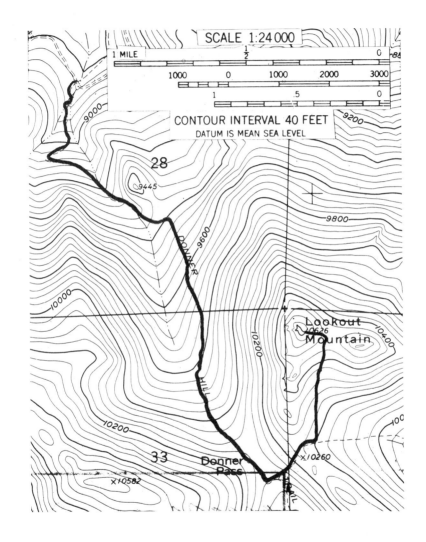

SCALE 1:24000

CONTOUR INTERVAL 40 FEET
DATUM IS MEAN SEA LEVEL

Most of the three-mile hike is through the forest. The trail zigzags uphill and joins an abandoned logging road. Climb along the old road past a slash pile and turn left (southeast) into the trees. Continue climbing to Donner Pass and a four-way trail junction.

To reach Lookout Mountain, which is not seen from the trail, take the Sheep Creek Trail branch for about two-tenths of a mile. Near a high point, cut left (north) into the trees. Watch for old tree blazes that lead toward Lookout Mountain. When the mountain comes into view, the marked trees give out, and the rest of the trip is cross-country.

Lookout Mountain is like a tripod. The first leg of the peak to come into view is below the summit and to the right. A small saddle separates the two peaks. Work your way to a saddle and the third leg of the tripod. From the saddle, scramble over downed timber and up a talus slope formed by the sluffing away of rotten granite.

It is a 1,786-foot climb to the summit of Lookout Mountain. No dependable source of water is available along the trail. Allow two hours to make the trip one way.

West White Pine Mountain

At the end of the West White Pine Mountain trail, there is a panoramic view of the Mummy Range, Crown Point, the Snowy Range in Wyoming, the Bald Mountains near Red Feather, the Rawahs, Lookout Mountain, the Signal Mountains, and East White Pine Mountain.

The trail heads a little past the Buckhorn Ranger Station on the right (north) side of the road. (Directions to the Buckhorn Road are given in Lookout Mountain.) Once the Buckhorn Road is reached, stay on it for 11.5 miles to the trailhead. Parking is available off the road.

Because most of the hike is in the montane zone, deer, elk, and grouse are frequently seen on the slopes of the

Aspen along the trail to West White Pine Mountain

West White Pine Mountain from East White Pine Mountain

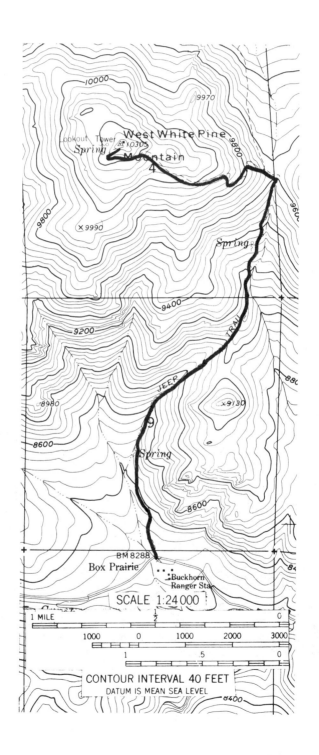

West White Pine
Mountain

Lookout Tower
Spring
X 0305

10000

9970

9800

X 9990

9600

Spring

9400

9200

JEEP TRAIL

X 9130

8980

8600

Spring

8600

BM 8288
Box Prairie

Buckhorn
Ranger Sta.

SCALE 1:24 000

1 MILE

1000   0   1000   2000   3000

1   .5   0

CONTOUR INTERVAL 40 FEET
DATUM IS MEAN SEA LEVEL

8400

44

West White Pine Mountain

mountain. In June, wildflowers bloom profusely. It is a migration route for many of the high-mountain birds in the spring.

From the beginning of the trail to the summit, the trail climbs at a steady pace over an old jeep road. The elevation gain in 3.5 miles is 2,017 feet. The trail winds in and out of stands of pine and aspen and to a meadow with a small spring at one end. A short, steep climb into lodgepole pine leads to a saddle between East and West White Pine Mountains and a trail junction. Take the left junction for the final climb to the summit of West White Pine Mountain. Several small granite outcroppings border the trail. Rocks to the west of the summit make a nice place to sit and have lunch.

It is possible to climb to the summit of East White Pine Mountain by turning right at the East White Pine Mountain sign located at the saddle and working through rubble and trees to the summit. The summit is at a 10,248-foot elevation, and is therefore 57 feet lower than West White

Pine Mountain. Carry water, since none is available along the trail to either mountain.

Note: The trail to West White Pine Mountain may later be designated as a National Jeep Trail.

Donner Pass to North Signal Mountain

The trail is not heavily used from Donner Pass to North Signal Mountain and, in fact, in places the route is little more than a series of rock cairns and tree blazes. It is a dry trail with only one intermittent spring crossed in the five mile hike from Donner Pass. From the trailhead to North Signal, it is seven miles with an elevation gain of 2,422 feet. To reach the trail access, follow the direction under Lookout Mountain.

Hike two miles to Donner Pass and a four-way junction. Make a turn to the right (west) and climb through a dry forest.

Trail along Donner Pass

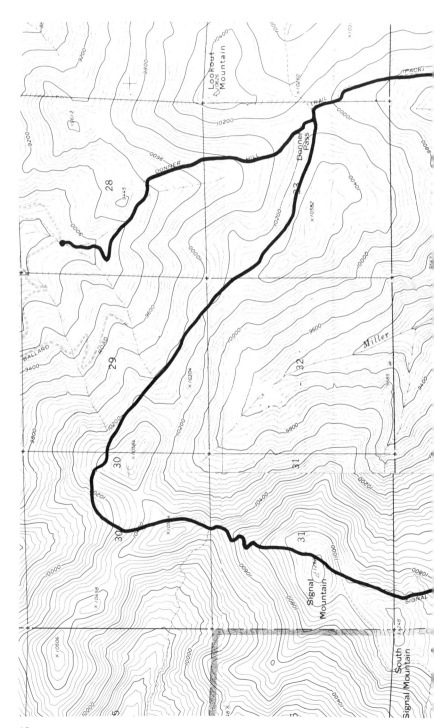

48

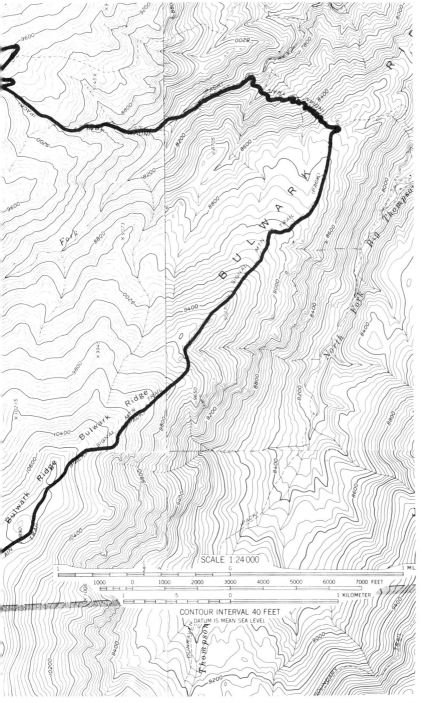

SCALE 1:24 000

CONTOUR INTERVAL 40 FEET
DATUM IS MEAN SEA LEVEL

49

Pass through an aging stand of trees, watching for tree blazes. Reach the top of a ridge and drop downhill following the contours of the hillside. The Signals can be seen through the trees as well as the ridge that must be climbed to reach the summit of North Signal.

Resume climbing to a trail junction and turn left to climb to a second trail junction and a sign 3.5 miles from Donner Pass. Bear left for the remaining 1.5 miles to North Signal, following a road to the Pennock Creek Junction. Turn left at the junction and hike uphill through a thick evergreen forest to North Signal Mountain.

The Signal Mountains were called Wolf Ridge by the Arapahoes, but named the Signals by white pioneers who thought they saw smoke signals coming from the summits.

It is possible to make a round trip from the Signals by hiking down Bulwark Ridge four miles to the Miller Fork junction, making a turn to the left (north) and dropping 915 feet in one mile to Miller Creek. At Miller Creek walk upstream for one mile to a faint trail junction marked by an upright post. Turn right (north) at the marker. For the next 3.5 miles, hike through a mixed pine forest, crossing two intermittent streams soon after leaving Miller Fork. Climb through a dry forest past a trail junction that comes in from the right. The trail winds past a pile of rocks with a nice view of Bulwark Ridge. For a time the trail is steep until it reaches two small meadows that are crossed in succession. Make two long switchbacks, cross a small spring, and hike through a dense forest to Donner Pass and the two mile hike back to the beginning of the trail. From Miller Fork to Donner Pass, there is an elevation gain of 2,400 feet. Total round trip mileage is 20.00 miles.

Lower Poudre River Canyon

Greyrock

Greyrock Mountain, located in the Cache La Poudre Canyon, is an easily accessible, popular hike. The torrential rains that hit the Big Thompson and Poudre watershed in July of 1976 changed the complex of the trail to Greyrock. Today the trail still meanders back and forth over the wash along the lower stretches of the trail. Trees have been uprooted and wrapped around larger trees, and rocks are stripped of protective soil, obliterating signs of the old trail.

To reach the trailhead, drive nine miles up the Poudre Canyon from Ted's Place and watch for a parking lot on the left side of the road. Immediately cross the Poudre River on a foot bridge and work along the river to the first bad wash from the north. Scramble over the debris and work back and forth over the wash to a bend in the trail and a trail sign. The trail to the left or west, leads to Greyrock Meadow, and the trail to the right, or north, leads to Greyrock Mountain. Turn right and head due north and hike uphill, following a draw. Near the head of the draw, hikers have caused considerable damage by trail cutting, and the rains in 1976 eroded much of the hillside along the cuts.

The trail winds through a rock cut and drops to a meadow at the base of Greyrock. Cross the meadow going northeast and pick up the trails that circles the southeast face of the mountain. Scramble over and around rocks and

Bobcat along Greyrock Trail

Greyrock Mountain and pond

Greyrock Mountain from Greyrock
Meadow

up three short switchbacks. Continue picking your way
through the rocks and wind below a steam granite face.
Snake uphill to some rock steps cut in the granite. Once
over the rock cut, stay right heading north over a flat
granite rock marked with cairns rather than left or south
over what appears to be a trail but is not.

Following the cairns, work toward the west over a granite outcropping to a small grassy depression that is sometimes filled with water. The trail circles the edge of the
meadow and then heads west through the rocks and trees.
It is well-marked with rock cairns. Before reaching the
small pond below Greyrock, the trail begins to bend south.

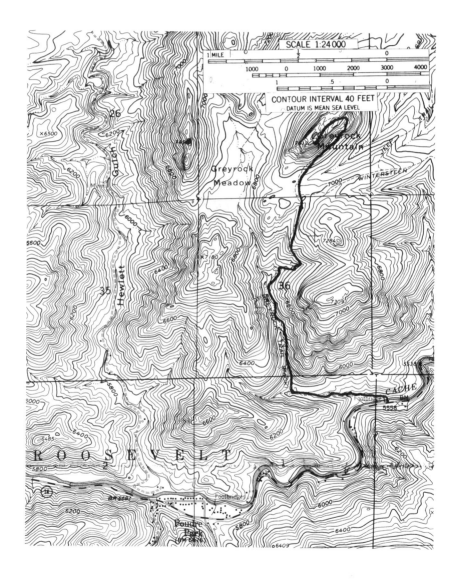

There is no inlet or outlet to the pond which is shallow. The water level is maintained by rainfall, seepage, and evaporation.

From the pond, it is a short scramble to Greyrock. Since the trail is open all year, it is best to make the three mile, 2,055 foot climb in the spring, fall, or winter. During the summer, it is usually too hot. From the summit, there is a view of the meadow below the peak. To the southeast is Fort Collins; to the east you can view the reservoir-dotted plains; to the southwest, west, and northwest lies the chain of Rocky Mountains. No drinking water is available along the trail. Because it is a steep three miles, allow two to three hours one way to make the hike.

It is now possible to follow the Greyrock Meadow trail and intercept the Greyrock Mountain trail, and from there climb to Greyrock Mountain. It makes a nice circle trip.

Hewlett Gulch

Hewlett Gulch makes an interesting walk that can be terminated any place. The hike starts on the Poudre River and follows Gordon Creek, a permanent stream that flows into the Poudre River. The hike is in the lower montane zone. A variety of grasses, deer browse plants, and ponderosa pine grow along the stream and on the hills. The trail is usually open all year.

To reach the trailhead, drive through Poudre Park on Colorado 14, 10.3 miles from the entrance to the canyon at Ted's Place and to the bridge at the west edge of Poudre Park that is over the Poudre River. This is a private bridge, so do not block the gate and driveway when you park. Cross the bridge and begin hiking along the right side of Gordon Creek through rabbitbrush and bitterbrush. The hills leading away from both sides of Gordon Creek change gradually. Several old foundations are scattered on both

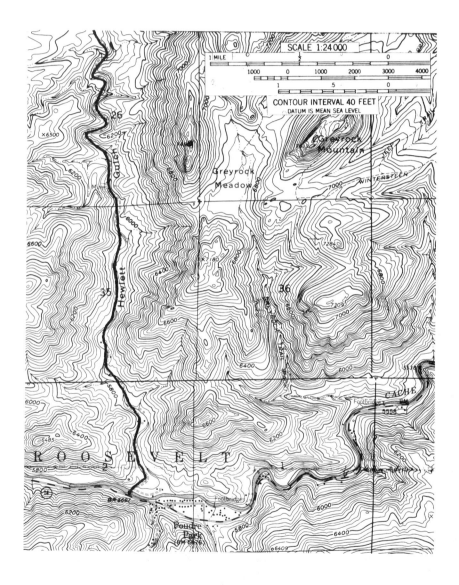

Hewlett Gulch Trail

Hewlett Gulch Trail

sides of the jeep trail, indicating a one-time sizable settlement. After leaving the decaying and crumbling foundations, the trail cuts through a narrow canyon with a pyramid-like peak on one side. Small ferns grow near the stream. The trail branches; take the right branch. The trail winds into a boxed canyon and around large rock outcroppings. The stream is crossed several times in succession. High, tree-covered ridges surround the canyon. At a trail branch, go left and leave the stream. When the trail reaches open range country, at about 3 miles with a 640 foot elevation gain, turn around and return to the Poudre River.

Youngs Gulch

The trail along the bottom of Youngs Gulch heads across the road from the Ansel Watrous Campground in the Poudre River Canyon, Colorado 14, 12.6 miles from the entrance to the canyon at Ted's Place. A small stream cuts through the draw with some forty crossings back and forth over the stream before the four-mile, one-way hike is completed. Although the trail never seems to climb, there is an elevation gain of 1,160 feet from start to finish. The entire hike is in the gulch among the trees common to the montane zone. Ponderosa pine is the characteristic tree with some Douglas fir, lodgepole pine, and aspen mixed in. Willow, alder, and Rocky Mountain maple grow along the stream. Rocky cliffs border the right side of the gulch. Above the ravine there are open hillsides. Part way up, the gulch divides. The left branch is hardly noticeable and continues to private property; the right or main branch turns and follows Prairie Gulch. For a time, the trail winds along the bottom of the narrow gulch, past an old mine, and finally into a broad meadow. At the meadow, the hike terminates when a fence and private property are reached. The water in the stream is not safe to drink.

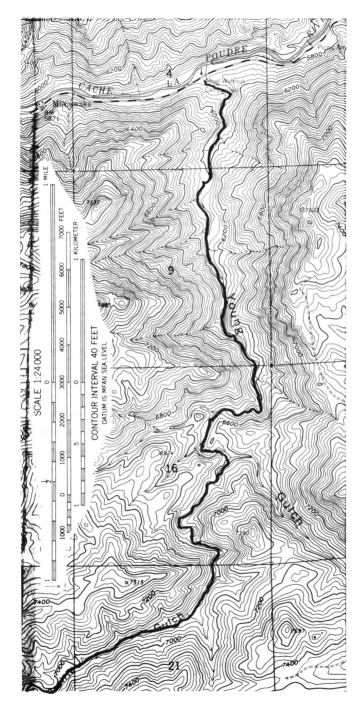

SCALE 1:24 000

CONTOUR INTERVAL 40 FEET
DATUM IS MEAN SEA LEVEL

Youngs Gulch Trail

Mount McConnel

Mount McConnel is a popular hike during the summer months. In the fall and winter, the trail is rarely used. The open sunny slopes to the summit are a haven for deer. Grouse reside in the trees, and coyotes leave their tracks in the snow that is protected by the trees. The circle hike, with an elevation gain of 1,200 feet, can be made in a half-day, but a pleasant spot at the high point on the trail makes it worthwhile to carry a lunch. Beautiful rock outcroppings are passed along the way to the summit.

The trail heads at the Fort Collins Mountain Recreation area on Colorado 14, 22.1 miles from the entrance to the canyon at Ted's Place. The entrance to the recreation area is closed in the winter, so park your car along the road. Walk over the bridge and past the trailers to the nature trail sign to start the hike. Climb through juniper, fir, and pine. As

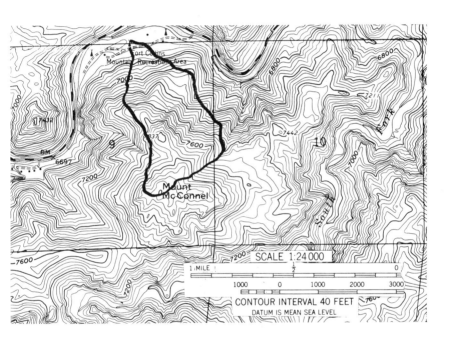

SCALE 1:24 000

1 MILE ½ 0

1000 0 1000 2000 3000

CONTOUR INTERVAL 40 FEET
DATUM IS MEAN SEA LEVEL

Mount McConnel Trail

Mt. McConnel Trail

Mt. McConnel Trail

the trail winds uphill, the Bald Mountains come into view. At the summit, a flat rock has been made into a picnic table. From the rock, West White Pine Mountain can be seen. The Mummy Range circles to the southwest, and Crown Point does not seem far away.

On the return trip, walk across the top of the mountain to a tree blaze and wander downhill past several rock cairns toward a deep ravine. Turn north at an overlook above the ravine. The ravine is paralleled for a time before cutting past a small knoll and over a saddle. After crossing the saddle, the trail is steep and drops quickly to a trail branch. The left branch eventually rejoins the main trail and passes through some of the more interesting scenery on the trail. The right branch continues to the Poudre River and the campground. No drinking water is available along the five-mile loop trail.

South Fork of the Poudre River

Identification of plants and shrubs is difficult with the disappearance of flowers and leaves. However, life zones being hiked help in identifying plants. The short trail that leads from the Cache La Poudre River to the South Fork is through the foothills zone with an altitude range of 6,500 to 7,500 feet. Most of the tress and shrubs common to this zone are found along the trail.

The trail access is 24.1 miles from Ted's Place on Colorado 14 or two miles from Fort Collins Recreation Area. To reach the trail, it is necessary to cross a bridge and walk between the two cabins to the east. The cabins are on forest service land. Once the trail is reached, it follows a draw to a small saddle. On the way, rock cliffs are passed. The left or west slopes of the hills are covered with widely spaced ponderosa pine and juniper. Sagebrush, mountain mahogany, antelopebrush, and kinnikinnic make up the

South Fork, Cache La Poudre River Trail

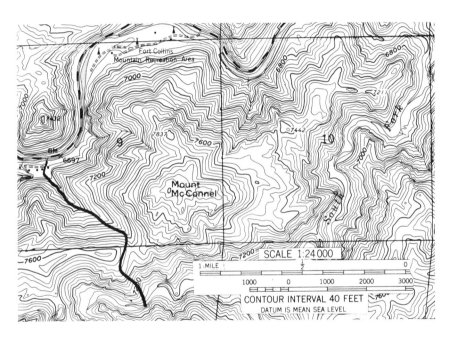

Fort Collins
Mountain Recreation Area

7000

7442

9

7837

7600

10

7442

6800

6800

South Fork

7000

BM
6697

7200

Mount
McConnel

7600

7200

SCALE 1:24 000

1 MILE   ½   0

1000   0   1000   2000   3000

CONTOUR INTERVAL 40 FEET
DATUM IS MEAN SEA LEVEL

7600

7600

South Fork, Cache La Poudre River Trail

undergrowth. The east slopes are cooler and support Douglas fir. Along the bottom of the draw, aspen and mountain maple are the predominant trees.

From the saddle, the deeply cut canyon of the South Fork can be seen. The river looks like a white ribbon dropped at random into the steep-walled canyon. Bear left at the saddle for about 100 yards and pick your way down the unimproved trail through brush, rock, grass, and cacti, with a few fir, ponderosa pine, and juniper growing in moisture depressions. Because of the browse, the hillside is an excellent place to watch for deer. Come to a pocket between the cliffs, and reach the river. In the winter when the river is frozen, it is possible to follow it for several miles downstream to Colorado 14. In the spring and summer, it is nearly impossible because of the steep-walled, narrow canyon that makes it necessary to cross the stream several times.

To vary the return trip, walk upstream and around a rock

outcropping with an interesting gendarme. Just past the cliff, look uphill and pick out a cut in a rock face. Head for the cut, but stay to the right of a long draw. Work up a steep slope that leads to the saddle and trail. Carry water. It is approximately 2 miles to the South Fork with an elevation gain of 903 feet and a loss of 500 feet.

Pingree Park Road and Middle Poudre River Canyon

Fish Creek

Fish Creek is a small quiet stream that heads east of Crown Point and flows into the South Fork. A lightly traveled trail follows the stream for several miles to some beaver ponds.

To reach the trail, drive Colorado 14 to the Pingree Park Road. Turn onto the Pingree Park Road and drive about nine miles to a cattleguard. Park along the road. Begin hiking on the right (south) side of the road. Work uphill in a southern direction. Then turn west and climb uphill past some outcroppings. Continue heading west through mahogany and pine until you reach the junction with Little Beaver Creek. At the junction take the trail that heads southwest and drops downhill to Fish Creek.

The trail winds, twists, and bends along the stream through open parks, into heavy stands of trees, and in and out of rocks, eventually reaching the beaver ponds. Aspen becomes the predominant tree.

Near a hard core of granite, the trail branches. One fork bends north away from Fish Creek and follows an intermittent stream uphill through a heavy stand of trees to a small saddle. The other branch continues along the stream past the ponds.

It is 6.5 miles to the trail branch at the granite outcropping with an elevation gain of 1,040 feet. This makes a good turn around point.

It is possible to cross the stream here and climb south to come out at the Sky Ranch Parking area where you can have someone pick you up. This adds about 1.3 miles to the 6.5 miles and another 200 feet of elevation gain.

Beaver dams on Fish Creek

Stormy Peaks from Fish Creek Trail

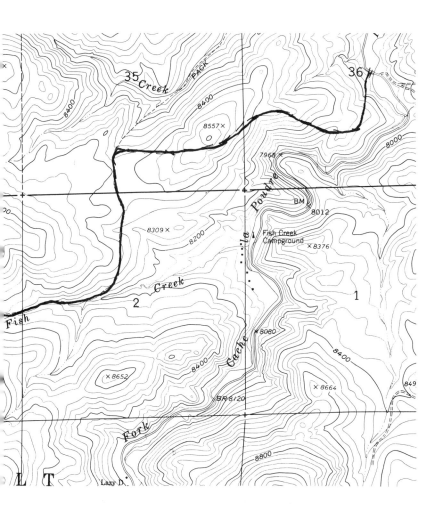

35 Creek

36

Fish

Creek

Fish Creek
Campground

Lazy D

L T

The trail winds, twists, and bends along the stream through open parks, into heavy stands of trees, and in and out of rocks, eventually reaching the beaver ponds. Aspen becomes the predominant tree. Small brook trout reside in the ponds.

Near a hard core of granite, the trail branches. One fork bends north away from Fish Creek and follows an intermittent stream uphill through a heavy stand of trees to a small saddle. The other branch continues along the stream past the ponds.

It is four miles to the trail branch at the granite outcropping with an elevation gain of 1,040 feet. Because the stream may be unsafe, carry water.

Note: Eventually, the Forest Service plans to join Fish Creek and Little Beaver Creek with a trail from the headwaters of Fish Creek over a divide to Little Beaver Creek.

Little Beaver Creek

The hike along the Old Flowers Road to Beaver Park with a return by way of Little Beaver Creek makes a pleasant loop trip of about ten miles. The elevation gain is 1,060 feet with a loss of 200 feet just before reaching Beaver Park.

To reach the trail, take Colorado 14 to the Pingree Park Road. Proceed on the Pingree Park Road 6.0 miles to U.S. Forest Service Road 152 and turn right (west) onto it. Continue 1.7 miles to a road junction below Bedspring Springs and park, as you come out at this point on the return trip. From the spring that is to the left of the road, take the old logging road and work in and out of forest and meadow and over knolls to a sign that points to the Flowers Trail. Wind uphill

Trail to Beaver Park

Beaver Park, Beaver Creek Trail

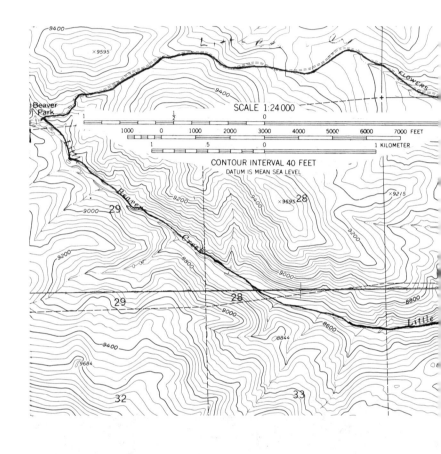

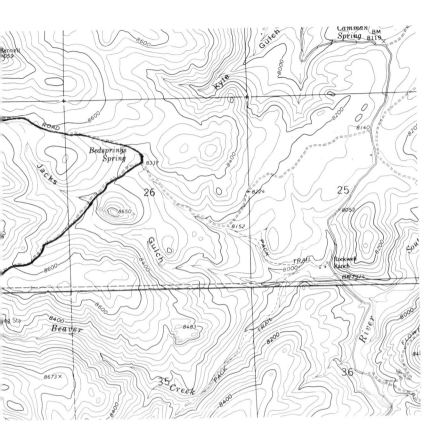

into a heavy pine forest and climb steadily to the high point on the trail. Drop to Beaver Park and the beginning of the Flowers Trail. Crown Point is framed between the trees on the way to Beaver Park, which is filled with several old beaver ponds. A small stream falls into the beaver ponds from the left.

From Beaver Park, it is possible to continue seven miles to the Browns Lake Trail, ten miles to Beaver Creek Trail, and 15 miles to Big South Fork on the Poudre River. On the return trip, follow the trail along Little Beaver Creek below the beaver ponds. Do not cross the stream but stay on the north side. Beautiful Colorado blue spruce mixed with willows, alder, and water birch shade the stream. Here and there on the dry hillsides, the beautiful mountain ball cacti grow. The canyon narrows before the trail joins a jeep track. Follow the jeep road, turning left (north) at a road junction, and switchback uphill out of the Little Beaver Creek canyon. Come to a gate and pass through private land, staying on the forest service access road. Wind above a meadow, past a small mountain, and across a stream. Rejoin the Old Flowers Road.

Dadd Gulch

Dadd Gulch is actually a jeep and stock trail. The trail provides a nice hike to the Crown Point Road from the Poudre River. It heads at the bridge about three-quarters of a mile east of Indian Meadows Resort, or 28.4 miles from Ted's Place at the entrance to Cache la Poudre Canyon and Colorado 14. Watch for a power station and a corral on the south side of the road. Parking is available at the picnic area across the bridge from the power station or on the road leading to the corral. Pass through the corral gate.

Trail along Dadd Gulch

Trail along Dadd Gulch

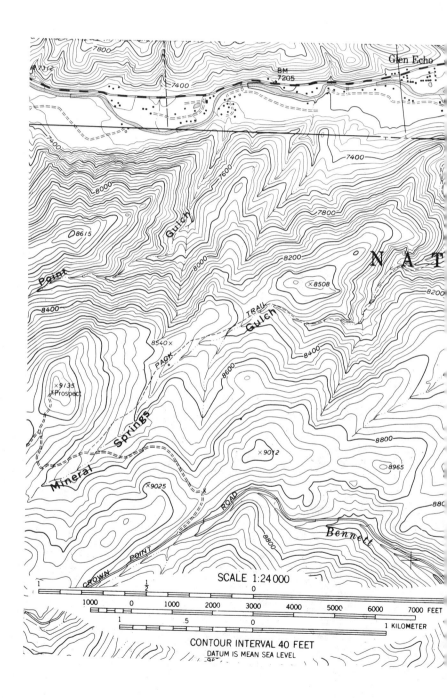

SCALE 1:24 000

CONTOUR INTERVAL 40 FEET
DATUM IS MEAN SEA LEVEL

78

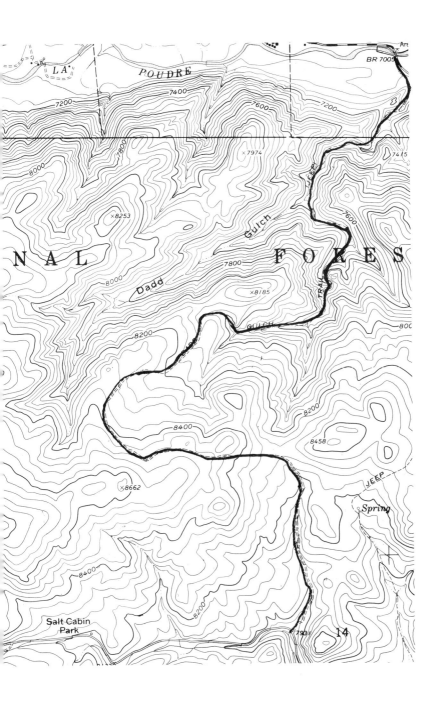

A small stream cuts through the gulch in the spring of the year. From the Poudre River to Crown Point Road, there is an elevation gain of 1,400 feet in 5 miles. The trail follows the stream much of the way, crossing it several times. In the spring of the year, the heart-leafed arnica, white Canada violet, lily of the valley, pussytoes, mallow, senecio, and mimulus color the banks of the stream. Power lines bisect the trail at one point and offer an alternate route, but because you will be going uphill, it is easier to stay on the jeep track. The rock formations in the gulch add interest to the hike. Because the trail follows the stream, the gulch remains relatively cool even on hot days. Soft breezes carry the sweet vanilla scent of the ponderosa pine and the wildflowers change as elevation is gained. The vegetation provides browse for deer and elk, and wild turkeys can occasionally be seen roosting in the trees. Carry water.

Mineral Springs Gulch

Mineral Springs Gulch heads across the Poudre River from Rustic, 31.2 miles from Ted's Place at the entrance to Poudre Canyon. An intermittent stream flows through a deep canyon. Along the way, several grotesque but spectacular rock formations are passed. The trail ends at the Crown Point Road or on the summit of 9,135-foot high Prospect Mountain.

To reach the trail, drive through Rustic heading west. Watch for the first bridge to the left (south) of the highway that crosses the river. Since this bridge and the road leading to the trail are private, park along the highway and cross the bridge on foot. Turn left (east) and walk six-tenths of a mile to the trailhead which is on the right (south) side of the private road. The distance to Mineral Springs is three miles. For a time the trail winds above a draw that carries water in the spring. Gradually bend away from the draw and intercept a jeep road. Follow the jeep road to the

Mineral Springs Gulch Trail

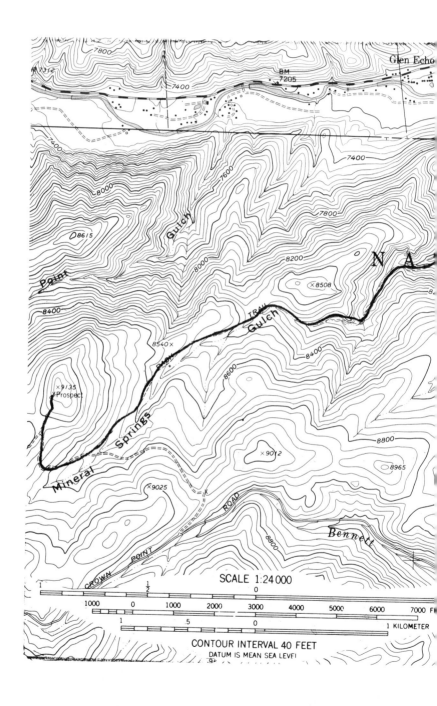

SCALE 1:24 000

CONTOUR INTERVAL 40 FEET
DATUM IS MEAN SEA LEVEL

LA·

POUDRE

7400

7200

7600

7200

BR 7005

×7974

7415

8000

×8253

Gulch

FORES

JEEP

7600

NAL

Dadd

7800

8000

TRAIL

×8185

GULCH

800

8200

DADD

8200

8400

8458

×8662

JEEP

Spring

8400

JEEP

8200

Salt Cabin
Park

7931

14

Mineral Springs Gulch Trail — Prospect Mountain

Mineral Springs Gulch Trail

Springs. The spring is a nice place to stop for lunch but do not drink the water. Carry your own.

After leaving the springs take the first road branch and go right (west). Climb steadily for the next three-quarters of a mile to a second fork in the road and again stay right. The left branch dead-ends at about one-half mile. Follow the right branch to the summit of Prospect Mountain; it rewards the hiker with a view of Rustic, the Poudre River, and snow-capped peaks in every direction.

To hike to the Crown Point Road, return to the first road junction beyond the springs and turn east. The road leads to the Crown Point Road and the Prospect Mountain sign. The elevation gain to Prospect Mountain is 1,935 feet, and to Crown Point Road, 1,600 feet.

Crown Point Road

Browns Lake

The trail to Browns Lake and Timberline Lake is a superb tundra hike. The entire trail is at an altitude between 10,000 and 12,000 feet. To reach the trail, drive 25.7 miles from Ted's Place at the entrance to Poudre Canyon (Colorado 14) to the Pingree Park Road. Proceed 4 miles to the Crown Point Road and turn right. Drive 12 miles to the Browns

Trail access to Browns Lake

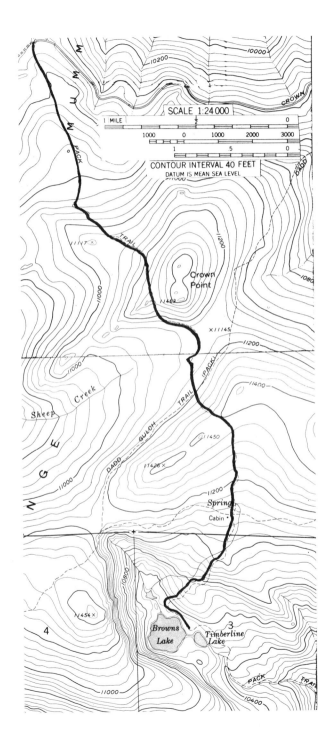

SCALE 1:24 000

CONTOUR INTERVAL 40 FEET
DATUM IS MEAN SEA LEVEL

Trail to Browns Lake

Trail to Browns Lake

Browns Lake

Lake trail sign on the left side of the road. The trail is a very rough jeep road that winds through a sparsely growing stand of limber pine and alpine fir and over a high rocky ridge. Snow stays on the ground late into the summer. Beautiful alpine flowers add color to the gray tundra. They change by the week as the snow recedes.

The trail reaches a high point and parallels Crown Peak through a tundra valley. There is a second climb over a ridge before the drop into Browns Lake. A cabin and spring is passed before the descent is reached. From the ridge, the steep-walled cirque above the lakes comes into view. The Old Flowers Trail bisects the Browns Lake Trail near the cabin. To reach the lakes continue downhill (south) to the shore of Browns Lake. Timberline Lake, the smaller of the two lakes, is east of Browns Lake.

Allow two hours one way to make the 4 mile hike. The first dependable source of water is at the spring near the cabin. There is a 720 foot elevation gain and a 780 foot loss to the lake.

Sheep Creek Reservoir and
Zimmerman Trail

Sheep Creek Reservoir has been abandoned for many years. Today the bottom of the reservoir is a lush, green meadow with Sheep Creek meandering through it. Willow is beginning to grow along the banks of the stream in the upper end of the meadow. A beautiful forest grows to the edge of the one-time lake. Elk and deer frequently come into the meadow. The face of the dam, the log tower with the control gate, a few crumbling cabins, and rusting scoop shovels are all that remain at the site.

To reach the trail, follow the directions given in the Browns Lake section. When you reach Crown Point Road, turn right. Drive another two miles to the trail access. There is no sign indicating the trail. Watch for a wide spot in the road just before entering a logged area. The trail takes off to the left.

Remains of Sheep Reservoir

Cabin along trail to Sheep Reservoir

Drop quickly into the valley holding Sheep Reservoir. After the downhill trek, the trail levels and enters a wet meadow. It is faint in places but picks up again back in the trees. Shortly after crossing the meadow, the trail branches. Take the left branch to Sheep Creek Reservoir. At the reservoir, cross the wood, rock, and earth dam and pass the cabins to reach Sheep Creek and a pleasant spot for lunch.

On the return trip, it is possible to follow the Zimmerman Trail to the Poudre River and have someone pick you up. To reach the trail, hike back to the trail junction and turn left for the 5 mile hike to the river. The trail is not heavily used and is hard to follow, but it is marked with tree blazes. Climb over a small divide and through an old burn area that is filling with a doghair stand of lodgepole pine. At a park-like area, the trail disappears. Cut straight across the park to a grove of aspen and watch for trail blazes. Once across the park, drop slowly through pine and glacial rubble. At an ancient lake site now being taken over by willow, the trail again becomes faint and hard to follow. Resort to the tree markings to find the way.

From this point, the trail follows a stream. As the canyon narrows, the stream must be crossed ten times before reaching the Poudre River. The crossings are made on logs, broken bridges, and stones, or by jumps, but none are difficult at normal stream flow. The trail comes out below the Colorado State Fish Hatchery. Cross a bridge and walk past a private lodge. Trespassing is allowed if you stay on the trail. The trail comes out on Colorado 14, 45.2 miles from Ted's Place at the entrance to the Poudre River Canyon. You can be met at the public parking space provided for fishermen. As a courtesy to the people at the lodge, you can report to them that you are coming from the trail.

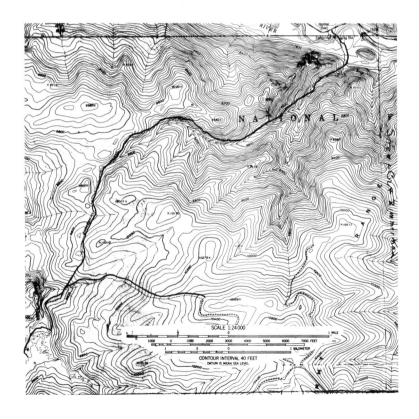

Pingree Park Road

North Signal Mountain

North and South Signal Mountains supposedly were given those names because the Indians at one time sent smoke signals from their summits. North Signal Mountain, with an elevation of 11,262 feet, is located next to the northeast boundary of Rocky Mountain National Park in Roosevelt National Forest. South Signal Mountain is inside the park. To reach the trail to North Signal Mountain, drive 12 miles on the Pingree Park Road from its junction with

Summit of North Signal Mountain

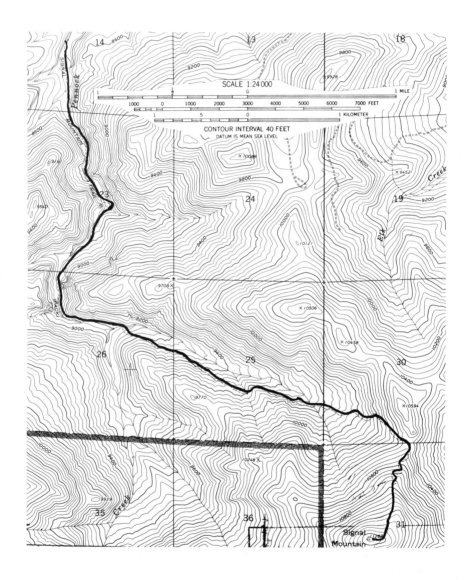

SCALE 1:24 000

CONTOUR INTERVAL 40 FEET
DATUM IS MEAN SEA LEVEL

Colorado 14. It is 25.7 miles from Ted's Place at the entrance to Poudre Canyon to the Pingree Park Road. The trail heads on the east side of the road.

The trail crosses a small stream and winds around a steep bank before coming to Pennock Creek. After walking along a road for a short distance, cross Pennock Creek and walk by a building and a flume. The trail follows Pennock Creek for some distance. Rock cliffs border one side of the stream. Several feeder streams are crossed along the way. Eventually the trail branches away from Pennock Creek and follows a tributary stream through a dense forest. After a

Pillar along Pennock Creek

steep uphill twist, a granite pinnacle is rounded and a jeep trail intercepted. By turning left, Lookout Mountain can be reached. The North Signal Mountain trail goes right. Cross an open park, go into the trees, and up an open slope that leads to the summit. South Signal Mountain is about a one-mile trek to the south. There is a 2,860 foot elevation gain in 7 miles to North Signal Mountain.

Mummy Pass

It is said that the Mummy Mountains resemble an Egyptian mummy lying on its back. When you are driving toward Pingree Park, there are places where the range does look like a mummy. The spectacular range includes Chapin, Chiquita, Ypsilon, Fairchild, Mummy, Hague, the Rowes, and Dunraven Mountains; these were called "White Owls" by the Arapahoes. The name was changed by either the Earl of Dunraven or William Hallett, a rancher in Estes Park.

A hike to Mummy Pass is a remote, quiet trail that leads into a large mountain valley. Mirror Lake can be reached from the pass. The trail heads near the Tom Bennett Campground on the Pingree Park Road. (Directions for reaching the Tom Bennett Campground are given under the Emmaline and Cirque Lakes section.)

Once the campground is reached, drive through it to the Cirque Lake sign. If you do not have a four-wheel-drive vehicle, park here and begin the hike. The first 2.2 miles are along the dirt road through an evergreen forest. After crossing Fall Creek, walk a short distance to the Mummy Pass, Mirror Lake trail sign on the left (south) side of the trail.

Leave the road and begin climbing through the forest, following a ridge that divides the Fall Creek and the South Fork of the Cache La Poudre River drainages. The trail alternates between steep climbs and short, level spots for

Trail to Mummy Pass

Trail to Mummy Pass

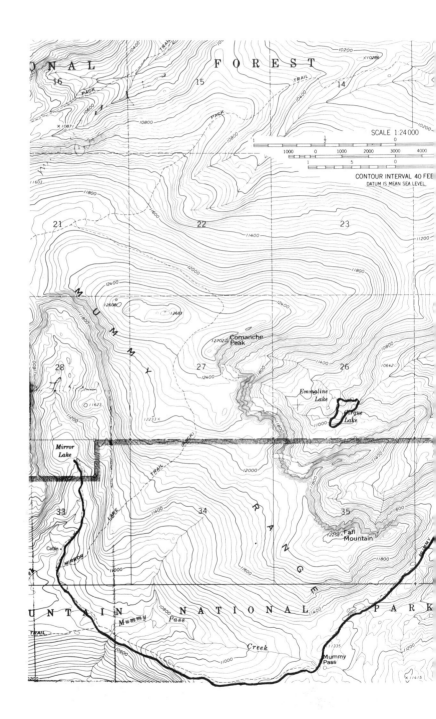

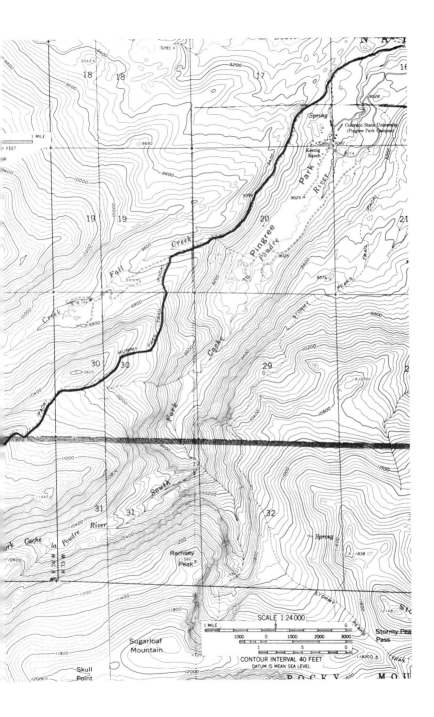

SCALE 1:24 000

1 MILE

1000   0   1000   2000   3000

1   5

CONTOUR INTERVAL 40 FEET
DATUM IS MEAN SEA LEVEL

about two miles. Here and there along the way, the Stormy Peaks and the South Fork come into view.

Pick up a branch of the South Fork after a long climb and climb toward a rock-pillared face. The trail winds uphill (southwest) into the alpine zone and enters Rocky Mountain National Park. Beaver Meadows and the huge glacial cirque that holds the Cirque Lakes comes into view near some large uprooted granite slabs. Twin Lakes and Greyrock can be picked out in the distance.

After a steep climb, level out on a bench that comes down from Fall Mountain and then forms a steep canyon wall of the South Fork. Walk across the bench through the tundra and drop southwest toward a snow-fed lake and a huge U-shaped valley filled with tarns and the headwaters of the South Fork. Cross an outlet of the small lake and wind through a minature rock-walled canyon to a second tarn. The trail continues to drop in elevation before beginning an easy climb to Mummy Pass.

From the Pass, the Mummy Mountains, the Never Summer Mountains, and the southern end of the Medicine Bow Mountains can be picked out. To the northwest is the steep-walled mountain cirque that holds Mirror Lake. On one side of the pass are the headwaters of the South Fork, and on the other, Mummy Pass Creek.

It is another three miles to Mirror Lake. The trail follows Mummy Pass Creek through an enormous glacier-carved valley. At the junction to Mirror Lake, turn right (northwest) and climb to the lake, going past a junction to the northeast that leads to Comanche Peak. It is possible to continue to Corral Park on the Long Draw Reservoir Road and have someone pick you up. There is an elevation gain of 2,480 feet and a loss of 240 feet to Mummy Pass.

Emmaline and Cirque Lakes

Emmaline Lake and Cirque Lake lie at the base of a glacier-filled cirque with Comanche Peak at one end. In addition to the lakes, there are several small tarns that dot the barren landscape. A rubble-filled slope connects Emmaline and Cirque Lakes. To reach the lakes, drive to the Tom Bennett Campground on the Pingree Park Road 16.1 miles from Colorado 14. Drive through the campground until you reach a sign to Sky Ranch. Take the left branch to Emmaline Lake and Cirque Meadows over a bad but passable road. However, without a truck or 4-wheel-drive vehicle, it is best to park and begin the five-mile hike along the road. For three and one-half miles follow the road with a crossing over Fall Creek and a walk through an evergreen forest to Cirque Meadow and a view of the cirque that holds the lakes. After the road ends, the trail begins past the remains of an old sawmill operation. New growth of spruce and fir is coming up in the area.

Emmaline Lake

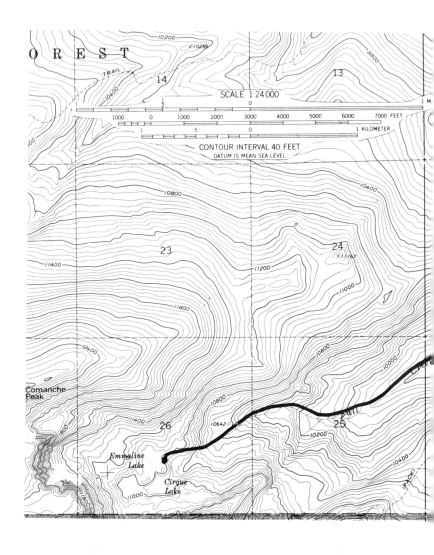

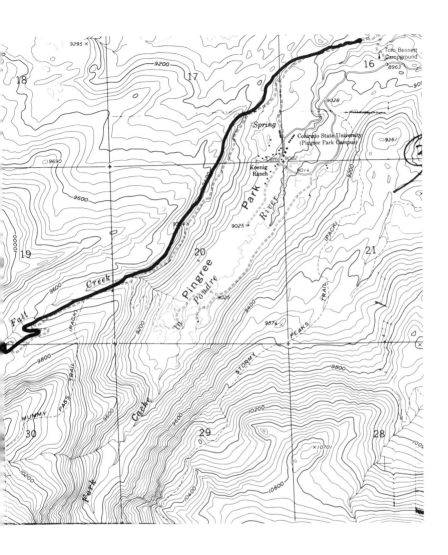

Cirque Lakes

Cirque Meadows

Cirque Lakes

The trail enters a mature stand of spruce and fir and follows the stream, gradually gaining in elevation until a talus slope is reached. From this point, it is a steady climb with several crossings over small streams. The waterfall from Emmaline Lake plunges over a granite face. Comanche Peak towers above the trail. Three glaciers are visible. The last part of the hike is through boulders and up a steep granite face. the entire basin holding the lakes and tarns is covered with flower rock gardens and picturesque, wind-twisted trees. It is a 2,063-foot elevation gain in five miles to Emmaline Lake.

Stormy Peaks Trail

The Stormy Peaks Trail access is a few hundred yards left (southeast) of the entrance to Pingree Park Campus, Colorado State University, 17.5 miles on the Pingree Park Road after the turn-off from Colorado 14. The hike to Stormy Peaks by this trail passes through a pleasant, quiet forest to a tundra meadow below the pass, and the stark, barren Stormy Peaks. It is approximately five miles to the pass and another one-half mile to the highest summit of the Stormy Peaks. The elevation gain is 3,120 feet.

By wandering around the pass, it is possible to see Lost Lake, Dunraven Lake, and Lake Louise below Rowe Mountain and Hagues Peak. The Stormy Peaks Trail can be followed to Lost Lake.

The first part of the trail follows a lateral moraine above the South Fork of the Cache La Poudre River. Along the way, there are views of the Mummy Range and Pingree Park. The trail is excellent to the Rocky Mountain National

Along the trail to Stormy Peaks

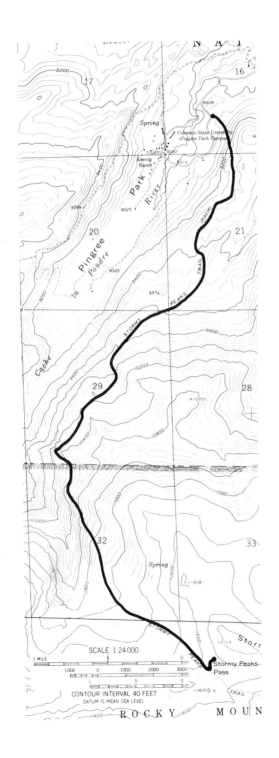

SCALE 1:24 000

1 MILE

1000 0 1000 2000 3000

1 5 0

CONTOUR INTERVAL 40 FEET
DATUM IS MEAN SEA LEVEL

107

Meadow below Stormy Peak

Park border. However, shortly after entering the park, the trail fades, and it is necessary to follow the rock cairns to the left of a large rock outcropping. Ramsey Peak and Sugarloaf Mountain can be seen across the canyon. From the rock outcropping, there are two ways to the pass. One trail cuts through the middle of an alpine meadow. The other wanders along the side of Stormy Peak.

The peaks surrounding the pass are barren and desolate, with huge boulders balanced one on top of another. The cirques between the mountains hold debris-littered snowfields that do not melt during the summer. Elk graze in the tundra. The higher of the two boulder summits of the Stormy Peaks is to the west and can be reached by scrambling up the rock and grass slope to the southeast.

Carry water because there is no dependable source along the trail. Allow three to four hours one way to make the hike.

Upper Poudre River Canyon

Roaring Creek Trail

Roaring Creek forms in the Nunn Creek Basin area of Roosevelt National Forest and drops swiftly through a forested canyon to the Poudre River. Mountain sheep frequently graze along the sides of the hills and in the willow-covered meadows. The trail heads east of the Roaring Creek culvert on Colorado 14, 39.9 miles from Ted's

Roaring Creek Trail

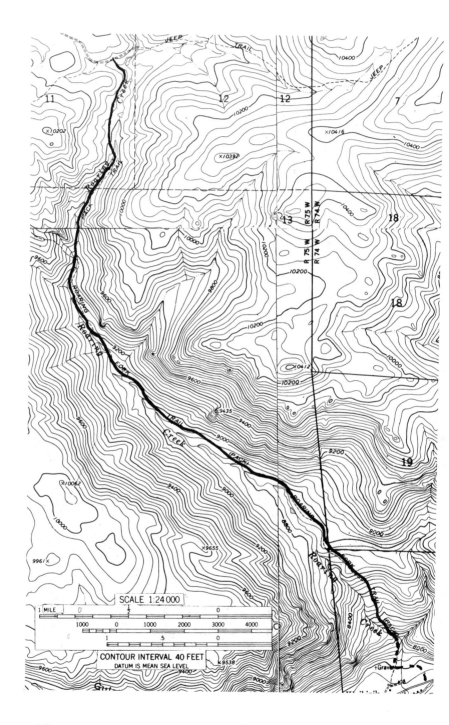

Mountain sheep on Roaring Creek Trail

Place at the entrance to Poudre Canyon, near a gravel area on the right (north) side of the road. Follow the trail that leads to the first stream crossing over a log bridge. Once across the stream, make six switchbacks. Follow the trail to another stream crossing and climb steeply before leveling out. Follow the stream for three or four miles through stands of aspen and lodgepole pine. Here and there the trail fades, but trees are marked to help pick up the trail. Eventually come to a possible bridge, cross and hike to a willow covered meadow. Continue along the stream to a junction with a jeep road. It is five miles to the South Bald Mountain jeep road with an elevation gain of 2,300 feet. The road makes a good turn-around point.

Chambers Lake Area

Blue Lake

Blue Lake is one of the more accessible destinations in the Rawah Wilderness located in Roosevelt National Forest. To reach the trailhead, drive 55 miles on Colorado 14 from the entrance to the Poudre Canyon to a parking area opposite the Long Draw Reservoir Road. The trail begins at the parking area. Proceed along the trail and come to Joe Wright Creek. Cross the stream on a bridge and follow the stream downhill to an old logging road. Turn left and follow the road, keeping right at the minor logging road junction. Round a bend to a breathtaking view of the peaks to the west. Leave the logging road and follow a trail to a crossing over Fall Creek. Wind through a dense evergreen forest to the entrance of the Rawah Wilderness. Continue walking through the forest to a small stream that cuts across the trail.

The trail proceeds at an erratic up and down pace across several stream draws before coming to an alpine meadow and a branch of Fall Creek. During the summer the meadow is filled with wildflowers that change by the month. Cross the stream and re-enter the trees and wind northwest uphill to a second meadow with several small springs. A short climb leads to a point above Blue Lake. To reach the lake drop 80 feet to the shoreline.

From the trail above Blue Lake, it is possible to climb west 320 feet along an outlet stream to Hang Lake, a small round lake at the base of a mountain ridge, or continue to

Blue Lake Pass

Blue Lake

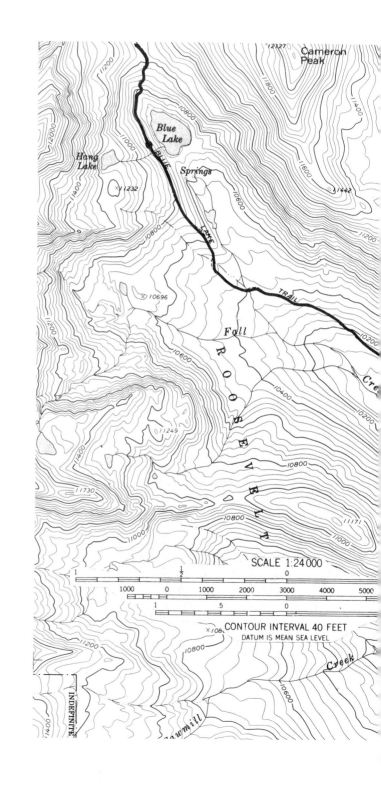

SCALE 1:24 000

1000   0   1000   2000   3000   4000   5000

CONTOUR INTERVAL 40 FEET
DATUM IS MEAN SEA LEVEL

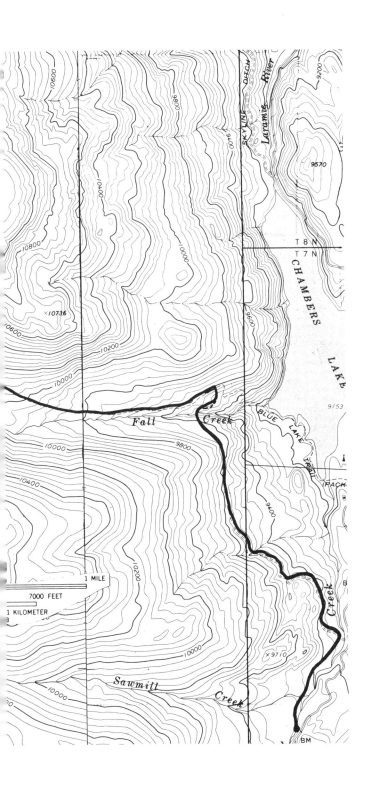

the pass above Blue Lake. The view of the Branch Lakes and Clarks Peak from the pass makes the climb worthwhile. From the pass it is possible to return by way of the West Branch and come out near the Tunnel Creek Campground. However, you must have someone pick you up since it is too far to walk back to the Chambers Lake Campground.

Twin Lakes

The trip to the Twin Lakes is a pleasant forest and meadow hike along a jeep road. After reaching the lakes, it is possible to continue along the road over the Green Ridge Trail as far as time allows in a one-day hike. There are two lakes, as the name implies, that are separated by a low hump. Cross-country, it is approximately one-half mile from East Twin Lake to West Twin Lake through a thick stand of pine. The total hike is 4 miles one way with an elevation gain of 100 feet.

To reach the trail, take the Woods Landing Road that turns right (north) off Colorado 14, 48.5 miles from Ted's Place at the entrance to Poudre Canyon. Drive around the east shore of Chambers Lake to a parking lot past Lost Lake. The jeep trail to Twin Lakes wanders around Lost Lake to a forest service outbuilding where the trail divides. Head right (northeast) and cross an intermittent stream. Climb uphill to Laramie Lake. The view across the clear waters of Laramie Lake to the mountains on the other side of Cameron Pass is spectacular with the Nokhu Crags near the Michigan Lakes as a backdrop.

After leaving Laramie Lake, the trail cuts along the edge of a musty-smelling swamp and in and out of a lodgepole pine forest and meadow following a lumpy ridge that is to the right (east). After crossing an intermittent stream, the road branches. The left branch (north) leads to West Twin Lake. The right branch which, also, heads north and slightly east, leads to East Twin Lake through a meadow and evergreen forest mixed with aspen. East Twin Lake is

Twin Lakes Trail

surrounded on the west and south sides by a swamp. The deeper part of the lake is to the north. A low rock promontory borders the east shore. From the north shore, the blue waters of the lake create a perfect backdrop for the grassy swamp and the blue snow-patched mountains in the distance.

To cross-country to West Twin Lake, return to the west side of the lake. Opposite an old beaver house, take a reading on your compass and cut through the trees at between 240° and 260° from north. There is a slight rise of 37 feet in the half-mile trek through a thick stand of evergreens. Come out in a meadow and pick up the jeep road that leads north to West Twin Lake. The lake lacks the promontory and lumpy ridge of East Twin Lake but is in a swampy depression.

From West Twin Lake, the jeep road climbs to the top of Green Ridge and follows the ridge for several miles, eventually crossing the Laramie-Poudre Tunnel, Nunn Creek, and Deadman Creek and ending at Deadman Road. From the ridge, the Rawahs are almost constantly in sight.

Note: This trail is being considered for National Jeep Trail designation.

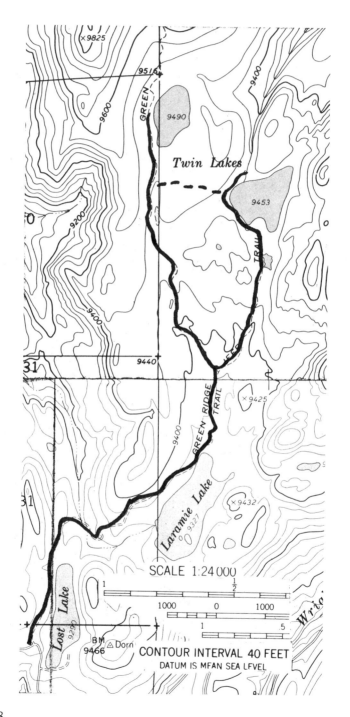

SCALE 1:24 000

CONTOUR INTERVAL 40 FEET
DATUM IS MEAN SEA LEVEL

Twin Lakes

Tunnel Creek Campground

Branch Lakes

The next three trails and lakes in this guide begin just north of the Tunnel Creek Campground on Woods Landing Road (Forest Route 190.) The Branch Lakes, the southern most lakes, are aptly named; they bear a close resemblance to a giant tree. Timber Lake to the southeast, Island Lake in the center, and Carey Lake to the north spread out like the limbs of a huge tree. The trail ends above Carey Lake. Island and Timber Lake are reached by cross-country hikes. Small tarns dot the landscape between the three lakes. The Medicine Bow Mountains form a steep, rocky backdrop for the clear lakes.

To reach the trailhead, drive 48.5 miles from Ted's Place on Colorado 14 to the Woods Landing junction. Turn north at the junction and drive another eight miles to the Tunnel Creek parking area a short distance north of the campground. The trail begins about 100 yards south of the parking area and then heads west along a road next to a ditch to a trail junction. At the junction turn left (south) and cross a bridge and wind through the trees to another trail junction. Take the right junction at the wilderness trail sign and begin hiking through a park-like stand of aspen and sage.

Climb gradually winding up several switchbacks that are spaced at intervals between long straight stretches and then drop downhill to the Rawah Wilderness Register and a drift fence. Resume an uphill hike and enter the wilderness. One mile past the wilderness boundary the trail

Carey Lake of the West Branch Lakes

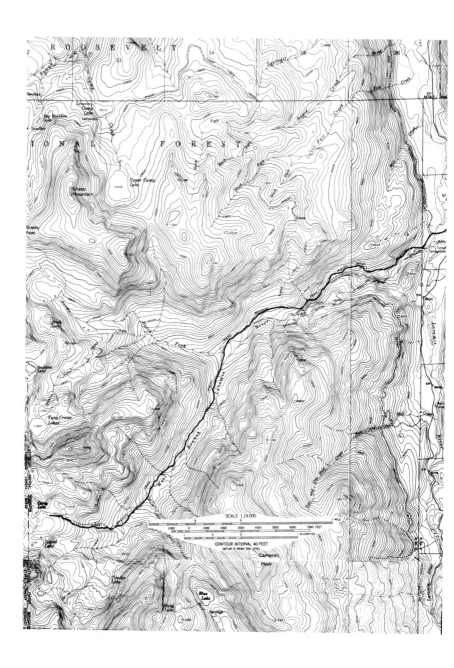

SCALE 1:24 000

CONTOUR INTERVAL 40 FEET
DATUM IS MEAN SEA LEVEL

Trail to West Branch Lakes

Island Lake, middle lake of the West Branch Lakes

branches. The left or main trail continues west above the West Branch of the Laramie River to a crossing over the North Fork.

After crossing the North Fork come to a trail junction and head left (south) to continue following the West Branch for another two miles to a third trail junction. The left or southeast junction leads to Blue Lake. The southwest junction continues to the Branch Lakes at a steady uphill pace with one crossing over a tributary to the West Branch and one crossing over the West Branch. The trail switchbacks uphill to the west following the West Branch to a point above Carey Lake.

Distances given on the forest service signs to Carey Lake contradict one another. From the sign at the parking area, it is seven miles to Carey Lake, but signs along the way add up to nine miles. Actual distance seems closer to eight miles. There is an elevation gain of 2,444 feet to Carey Lake. Use your discretion in drinking the water along the way.

Twin Crater Lakes

Many of the trails in the Rawah Wilderness are too long for a one-day hike. The two Crater Lakes that also begin near the Tunnel Creek Campground (with directions for reaching the trail head given under Branch Lakes) are six and one-half miles from the trail access, with an elevation gain of 2,403 feet, and are within the reach of most day hikers. The two lakes are divided by a narrow, low bridge of land. High ridges of the Medicine Bow Mountains tower above the lakes, and on a calm day, the permanent snow-fields are reflected in the waters of the lakes. To the north of Twin Crater Lakers, Rockhole Lake and Bench Lake are found. South Rawah Peak is to the north of the lakes. From the trail that leads to Twin Crater Lakes, a ribbon-like falls plunges over a steep cliff.

Trail to Twin Crater Lakes

Twin Crater Lakes

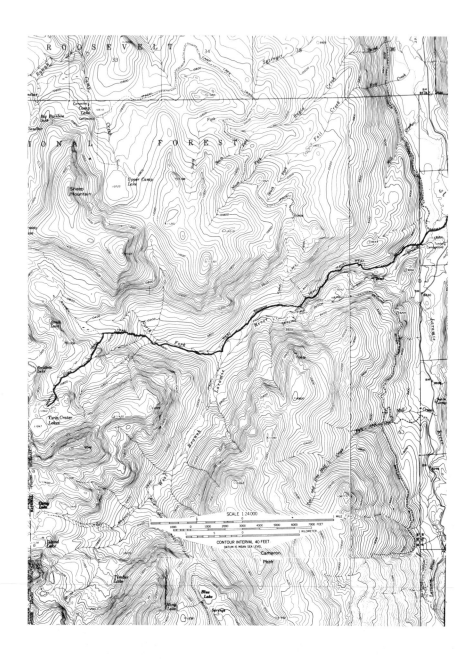

SCALE 1:24 000

CONTOUR INTERVAL 40 FEET
DATUM IS MEAN SEA LEVEL

Twin Crater Lake Trail, North fork

The first part of the trail follows the same route as that to the Branch Lakes. However, after crossing the North Fork, the trail branches a short distance beyond the bridge at the Rawah Lake sign. Instead of heading south along the West Branch, turn right (west) onto the Rawah Lake trail and work uphill following the North Fork to a log foot bridge over the North Fork. After recrossing the stream, climb uphill over several switchbacks to another trail junction. Turn left (south) and resume an uphill trek along a ridge through subalpine meadows, over small streams, boulder strewn terraces, and to the smaller of the Crater Lakes. Rockhole Lake is to the north of the Crater Lakes up a steep, rocky face.

Camp Lakes

Although it is a seven-mile hike to Lower Camp Lake, it is not difficult. Most of the climbing is done in the first four miles and then the trail levels out. There are two Camp Lakes located in the Rawah Wilderness that are called Lower Camp Lake and Upper Camp Lake. They are nestled at the base of Sheep Mountain.

The trail to the lakes, also, begins at the Tunnel Creek parking area (with directions for reaching the trailhead given under Branch Lakes). The first part of the trail is along the West Branch of the Laramie River and is the same route that is taken to the Branch Lakes and Twin Crater Lakes. About a mile past the Forest Service Register, take the trail that branches to the right (north) of the West Branch Trail and begin a steep climb over an unimproved trail.

Along the way, there are some zigzags in the trail, which follows the wilderness boundary. When the trail levels and

Lower Camp Lake

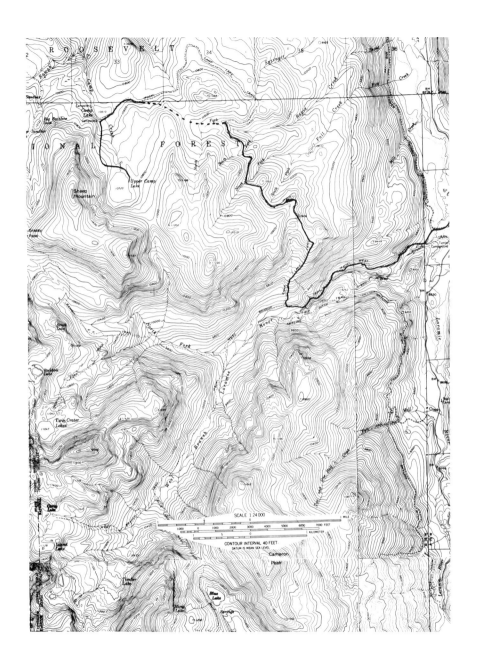

129

Upper Camp Lake

opens up, Cameron Peak, Blue Lake Pass, Clark Peak, four unnamed peaks, and the West Branch Canyon can be seen. Another short climb past the remains of old cabins brings you to the Skyline Ditch.

The Ditch which has been abandoned due to litigation over water rights with the State of Wyoming, is followed to a big bend. At the start of the bend, the trail branches to the left (west) and follows the North Fork of Rapid Creek. Here and there, the trail is faint and almost disappears. After leaving the North Fork, head to the northwest and watch for trail signs. Taking the shortcut, which is sanctioned by the Forest Service, saves about a mile of hiking and is more interesting than the main trail along the ditch. After rejoining the main trail, turn west and hike downhill to Lower Camp Lake.

To reach Upper Camp Lake, walk around the southern shore of Lower Camp Lake to a trail junction. The trail that continues north around the west side of the lake leads to the first of the Rawah Lakes and is an additional two miles of hiking. The left (south) junction follows Camp Creek for three-quarters of a mile to the upper lake through the beautiful subalpine zone. Just below the banks of Upper

Camp Lake, there is a small tarn and the headwaters of Camp Creek.

There is a total elevation gain of 2,123 feet to Upper Camp Lake. Allow four hours one way to make the hike. Drinking water is available along the trail.

Long Draw Reservoir

Big South Trail

(This was called Peterson Lake. Because the bridge over the Big South washed out, it is no longer possible to hike from Peterson Lake since it is extremely dangerous to cross the river by wading. The trail description should read as follows.)

The Big South Trail from Colorado 14 along the river is a forest hike. It is an easy hike of 6.5 miles with an elevation gain of 1,322 feet to the point where it leaves the river which is a good turn around place.

To reach the Big South Trailhead, drive 47.6 miles from Ted's Place at the entrance to the Poudre Canyon. There is parking available at the trailhead on the south side of the highway.

Begin hiking through an evergreen forest and cross several talus slopes. The river has several small falls and pools that are worth stopping to see. Follow the river about two miles to a crossing over May Creek. Continue walking up and down along the river that falls over giant rocks and creates natural pools where it is often possible to see trout. In the fall the aspen color the hills on both sides of the river. The canyon gradually widens before reaching the bend in the trail that heads east away from the river.

Note: If you chose to backpack, the trail climbs steeply uphill for approximately three miles to the Mirror Lake, Old Flowers trail junction. The Mirror Lake Trail branches south and then heads east up a long hill and follows the cirque that holds Mirror Lake. Continue uphill and around the west side of an

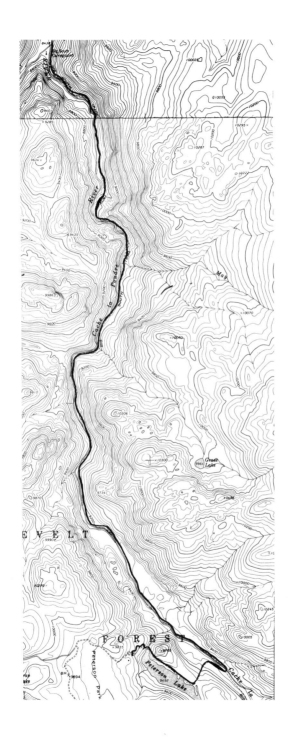

unnamed peak to the southwest of Comanche Peak. From here the trail drops downhill to a junction with the trail that leads one mile north to Mirror Lake. This adds about 11 miles and 2,640 feet to the above hike. You can come out at Corral Park and have someone pick you up by following the Mirror Lake Trail directions.

The Old Flowers junction can also be taken. Head east and cross the tundra to a fork in the trail above the headwaters of Beaver Creek. Going left (north) brings you out at Crown Point. Heading east brings you to an old cabin and the trail that follows Beaver Creek to Comanche Reservoir. This exits at Sky Ranch and adds about 11 miles of hiking to the Big South Trail and 1,560 feet of elevation gain.

If you exit at Crown Point or Sky Ranch you will need someone to pick you up.

Mirror Lake

Mirror Lake nestles on the west side of the Mummy Mountains; there is also another small, unnamed lake near it at an elevation of 11,040 feet. It is possible to reach these gem-like lakes from the Long Draw Reservoir Road. The hike involves seven miles of steep climbing one way. To reach the trailhead, drive past Chambers Lake to the Long Draw Reservoir turnoff on the left side of the road, 55 miles from Ted's Place at the entrance to Poudre Canyon. Drive 8 miles toward the reservoir, watching for the parking area on the left side of the road near Corral Park. The trail begins at Corral Creek, following the stream to its junction with La Poudre Pass Creek. Most of the hike is within Rocky Mountain National Park, including Mirror Lake. It is 7 miles with an elevation gain of 1,200 feet to the lake.

Two views of Mirror Lake

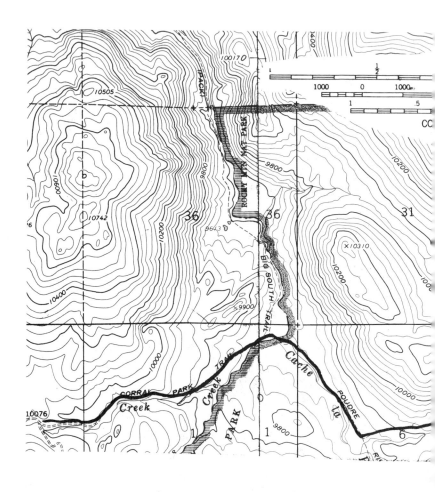

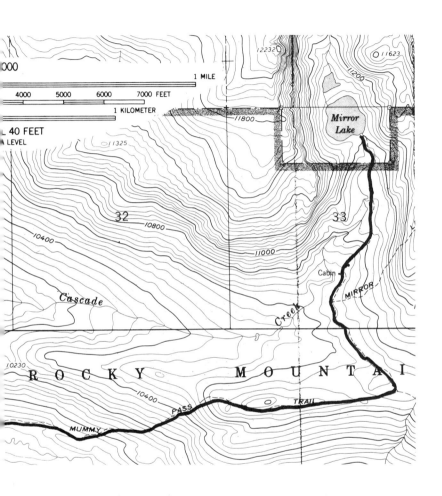

Tarn above Mirror Lake

Before reaching the Cache La Poudre River, the trail branches. The left (north) branch follows the Big South Trail. The right (southeast) continues to a bridge crossing over the river and enters the park. There is a short trek through a meadow and a crossing over Hague Creek. Then the trail heads east. It is a long climb up a lateral moraine through a mixed forest of pine, fir, and spruce with a heavy undergrowth of huckleberry. The trail reaches the crest of the ridge and continues to a second junction to Mummy Pass or Mirror Lake. Turn left (northwest) and continue following the trail to Cascade Creek that comes from Mirror Lake. The cirque holding Mirror Lake can be seen from a meadow. A small waterfall tumbles into the meadow at the far end. After leaving the meadow, the trail climbs through an old forest to the junction with Comanche Peak. Continue left (north) to Mirror Lake past a veil-like waterfall and over the terminal moraine that hold back the waters of the lake.

Unnamed mountain ridges rise perpendicularly on both sides of the lake. Eighty feet above the north end of Mirror Lake there is the second, very shallow, crystal lake resting below the fellfields. Looking south across Mirror Lake that hangs above huge valleys can be seen Flatiron Mountain and Desolation Peaks.

Colorado State Park

Montgomery Pass

Montgomery Pass located northwest of Cameron Pass makes a short but scenic hike of two miles one way. From the pass there are fantastic views of North Park and North Fork Michigan Creek Reservoir. It is 480 feet higher than Cameron Pass, and therefore, ends above timberline. The trail is actually a jeep road that is now closed by the new highway over Cameron Pass. Because of the new road it is difficult to locate the trail access which is no more than a tenth of a mile west of the western end of Joe Wright Reservoir.

From Ted's Place at the entrance to the Poudre Canyon on Colorado 14, it is 55 miles to the beginning of the trail. The trail starts on the north side of the road where a culvert transports the waters of Montgomery Creek under the highway to Joe Wright Creek. Parking is limited to the shoulders of the road.

The jeep track is easy to follow to the pass. It winds along Montgomery Creek for a short distance through a spruce, fir forest and between an old cabin and outbuilding. After walking by a small waterfall, the trail bends away from Montgomery Creek and begins heading west.

It is a steady climb along the road. One minor road comes in from the left at one point but stay on the main track. The trail bends and twists uphill through the thick evergreen forest and past small meadows that in the summer are filled with wildflowers.

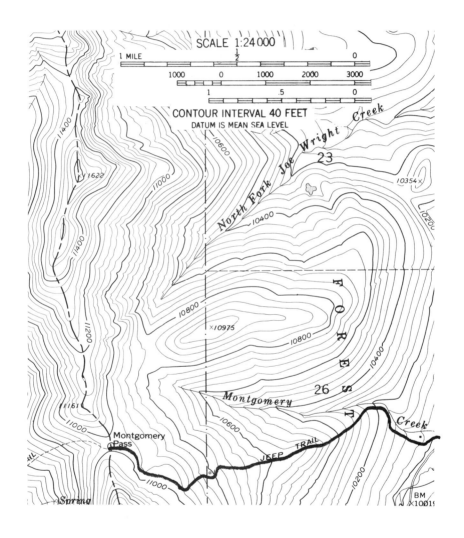

SCALE 1:24000

1 MILE $\frac{1}{2}$ 0

1000   0   1000   2000   3000

1   .5   0

CONTOUR INTERVAL 40 FEET
DATUM IS MEAN SEA LEVEL

Hike between an ancient cabin that is on the north side of the track and a series of abandoned mines on the south. West of the cabin the road winds above a marshy area with a permanent but small spring.

The trail becomes steeper and then drops to a crossing over a small stream. After crossing the stream resume climbing. Enter the alpine tundra and climb to Montgomery Pass which is marked by a Colorado State Forest sign. Watch for elk in the alpine meadows and golden eagles and hawks.

The jeep road continues to the north along the mountain ridges and then drops into North Park. Walking along the ridge makes a nice additional hike that leads over several unnamed mountains. From the ridge several peaks come into view including the impressive Nokhu Crags.

Allow 1 to 1½ hours one way for the 1,000-foot climb and carry water.

Snow Lake and Agnes Lake

In July, Snow Lake is still ice-covered and surrounded by snow. The barren, sharp-toothed Nokhu Crags form a semicircle around the lake that is in Colorado State Park on the west side of Cameron Pass. Just below Snow Lake are the two Michigan Lakes, sometimes called American Lakes, that form the headwaters of the Michigan River. After crossing Cameron Pass, drive to the Crags area in Colorado State Park and take the road to the left or south that leads to Agnes Lake and American Lakes. There is an entry fee into the State Park. Drive .9 miles into the State Park and turn left to drive to the trailhead to American Lakes and Snow Lake.

Snow Lake is not mentioned on the trail sign but it lies 320 feet above American Lakes. The distance to American Lakes is 4.2 miles with a 1,410 foot elevation gain. Begin hiking along the Michigan River over a badly eroded roadbed that is an abandoned logging road. From the trail the high jagged peaks are continually visible. The trail crosses the Michigan Ditch

Snow Lake

Static Peak near Snow Lake

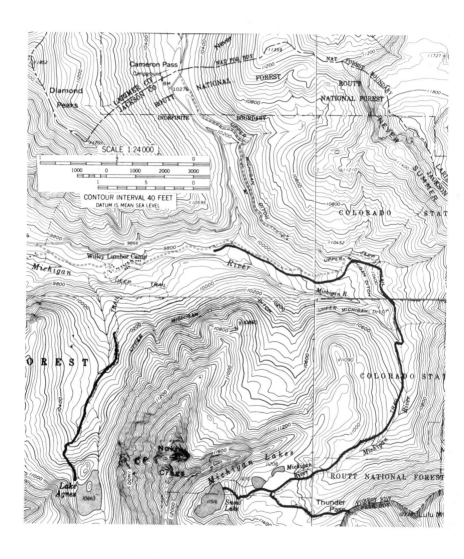

Peaks above Snow Lake

and winds below Iron Mountain and Thunder Mountain in the Never Summer Range to an abandoned sawmill and broken down shacks. The trail continues south following the Michigan River along the east bank and climbs through an old logged area to a campsite located in a grove of trees. Pass through the campsite and drop a few feet to a stream crossing. After crossing this stream the trail rejoins the jeep road. Begin a steep uphill climb along the road to an overlook of the American Lakes. Leave the road that continues to Thunder Pass and walk cross-country around the south shore of the lakes to a moraine rising above them. Climb the moraine to Snow Lake.

Because it is a short hike to Snow Lake taking about two hours one way, it is possible to leave Snow Lake and hike Thunder Pass, which is 1,530 feet elevation gain and five miles from the trailhead. From Thunder Pass, you can see Specimen Mountain, the Never Summer Mountains to the south and southwest, and Medicine Bow Mountains to the northwest.

For a shorter hike, Agnes Lake on the west side of the Crags is equally as beautiful as Snow Lake. To get to Agnes Lake follow the road to the parking lot. The lake is about one mile due south from the parking area up a steep rocky grade that follows the outlet stream from the lake. To reach the parking area continue south rather than turning east at the American Lake junction.

If time permits, you can do Snow Lake during the first part of the day and Agnes Lake during the second part of the day.

Note: On the return trip, the park has built a new trail that follows around the northwest shore of the American Lakes and then drops downhill past a fantastic rock glacier flowing from the Crags. The trail cuts below the moraine and continues to a road. Follow it to the ditch and a three-way junction. Make a turn to the west and continue to the parking area. It is 4 miles to the lakes from the parking area with an elevation gain of 1,210 feet.

North Fork of the Cache La Poudre River

Middle and South Bald Mountains

The hike to Middle and South Bald Mountains is a challenge to those who like to scout trails and to read maps and compasses. It is an easy trail to follow in places and an easy trail to lose in others, because much of the trail is through logged areas and over logging roads. The trail access is across the road from the North Fork Poudre Campground seven miles west of Red Feather Lakes on the Deadman Road. The elevation gain to Middle Bald is 1,842 feet in 6 miles.

The first part of the trail is wide and through a pine forest along Killpecker Creek. After a steady climb, a logged-over area is intercepted, and the trail is easy to lose. Trail markers from this point can be the standard forest service slash on a tree; red, blue, and yellow ribbons tied to limbs; or blue and red paint marks. Make a diagonal cut through the slash to a road. At the edge of the logged area and about 100 yards west of the stream, the trail begins again. Watch for a red splash of paint on a tall tree stump. Once the trail is picked up, it is easy to follow to a spring and the last available water on the trail. Soon the trail branches in every direction. Head west and then south to a ridge and another road and logged area. Walk south a short distance along the ridge and the road that cuts the edge of the logged area. Watch for a pole held up by rocks in the logged area. Begin climbing through the slash watching for ribbons and paint

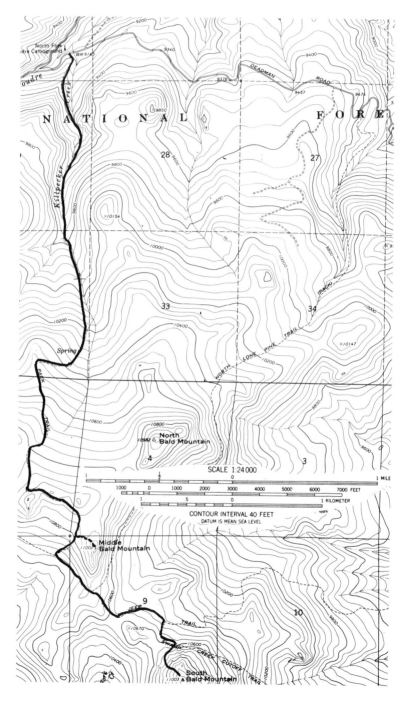

Killpecker Creek Trail to Middle Bald Mountain

Middle Bald Mountain

markers into the trees. Work uphill to a meadow. Poles mark the way through the meadow heading west. At the second pole, turn left (south) and enter the trees. By watching for new and old forest service tree marks, the trail is easy to follow. Climb south at a steady pace and then bend southeast into another meadow at the base of Middle Bald Mountain. It is a steep scramble over loose rubble to the summit and a view of the other two Bald Mountains.

From Middle Bald Mountain, it is approximately 1.5 miles to South Bald Mountain. Turn right or south in the meadow and follow the carins to the trees. Drop through the trees to a jeep road and turn left (southeast). Walk along the road to a branch in the road and take a sharp right turn for a climb up a steep grade. South Bald Mountain can be seen through the trees at the crest of the ridge. Drop into a large meadow below South Bald Mountain. To reach the summit, scramble over loose rubble. From the summit of the peak, the Rawahs, Mummy Range, Medicine Bow Mountains in Wyoming, Crown Point, and the Bald Mountains are seen.

North Lone Pine Trail
to North Bald Mountain

Of the three Bald Mountains southwest of Red Feather Lakes, North Bald Mountain has the most trees. It is also the lowest in elevation at 10,982 feet. The North Lone Pine Trail is a pleasant easy hike of three miles to the base of North Bald Mountain. To reach the trailhead, follow Deadman Road five miles past the turn-off to Red Feather Lakes. The trailhead is on the left side of the road at the corner of the fourth switchback of four long switchbacks on the Deadman Road. Just before turning north look for the jeep road that takes off to the southeast. There is parking just west of here at the trail access.

South Bald Mountain

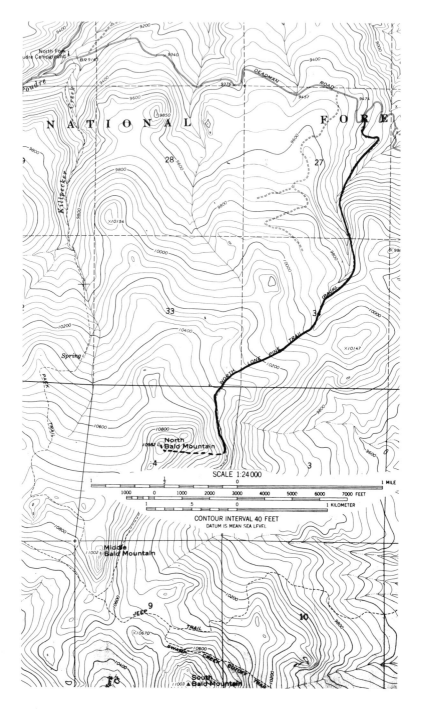

SCALE 1:24 000

CONTOUR INTERVAL 40 FEET
DATUM IS MEAN SEA LEVEL

Although much of North Lone Pine Trail is not heavily used, it is well-marked with forest service tree blazes. The first part of the trail follows a jeep road downhill in a southern direction. After dropping downhill toward Lone Pine Creek the Road branches to the right. Turn right (southwest) and walk through a mixed forest of spruce, pine, fir, and aspen with a ground cover of kinnikinnic, low growing juniper, duff, and wildflowers. After climbing at a slow pace, the jeep road passes a forest service experiment shed and crosses North Lone Pine Creek.

The jeep road continues to follow the stream through a meadow. Once through the meadow, stay on the east side of the stream. Very quickly cross the stream and for a short walk stay on the west side of North Lone Pine Creek to a third and last crossing. Climb gradually to the south following along the jeep road to a junction that comes in from the southeast and turn onto it.

For a time the trail winds to the southeast but then bends southwest and winds uphill. Continue southwest for a short downhill trek before resuming a climb. There is an opening in the trees for a quick glimpse of South Bald Mountain. Climb to a high point and a second view of the Bald Mountains near a pile of granite.

The trail descends the ridge and begins see-sawing south to the base of North Bald Mountain which cannot be seen through the trees. For a hike to the actual summit of North Bald Mountain, it is necessary to go cross-country and climb above the trail about 542 feet. After turning west and wandering along on level ground, you will come to a second view point of South and Middle Bald Mountains. This point is a good place to turn and begin the ascent of North Bald Mountain traveling in a northwest direction. It takes from thirty to forty minutes to reach the summit. Some rock outcroppings are the first indication that you are nearing the crest.

For the summit of North Bald Mountain you have a view of South and Middle Bald Mountains to the south, Black Mountain to the northeast, Red Feather Lakes and the Prairies to the east, and the Mummy Range in the distance.

View from North Bald Mountain

A word of caution on your descent of North Bald Mountain. Since the trail is faint, it is easy to miss it. Watch
carefully for the tree blazes and other land markings when
you come downhill.

The North Lone Pine Trail continues to Middle Bald
Mountain. Again the trail is marked with tree blazes. It
ends in a small meadow at the base of Middle Bald. Although the map indicates that the trail continues to a junction with the South Bald Mountain Trail, the author was
not able to locate that section of the trail. By climbing the
ridge that runs out from Middle Bald, it is possible to pick
up the Killpecker Trail and return to North Fork Poudre
Campground. It is a fair distance of four miles on the
Deadman Road back to the North Lone Pine Trail. There is
no water on the trail. The elevation gain to North Bald is
1,582 feet.

Addendum

Homestead Meadows Trail

In 1978, the U.S. Forest Service purchased land with monies from the Federal Land and Water Conservation Fund known as the Homestead Meadows. Since that date, trails have been developed into the area. The main trails take off from Lion Gulch.

To reach the trailhead, drive to Lyons, Colorado, and take U.S. 36 at the west end of town. Drive 12.3 miles to the parking space and trail located on the left (south) side of the road. Two small signs indicate "Lion Gulch" and "Trail."

The Lion Gulch Trail that leads into the Homestead Meadows Trail system follows routes used by the early pioneers who settled the area in the late 1800's. Several homes and buildings still stand, some in remarkable repair.

The Sawmill Loop and Meadow Loop lead to three homesteads, with a hiking distance round trip of eight miles and an elevation gain of 1,200 feet. The first part of the trail drops downhill about 300 yards to a bridge crossing over the Little Thompson River. After crossing the bridge turn right (west) onto a road and walk a short distance to pick up a trail to your left.

Begin climbing through a forest of spruce and fir and very shortly level out and cross a bridge over Lion Gulch. Resume climbing and as you leave the stream, make one switchback. Ponderosa pine shade squaw currant, dwarf juniper, kinnikinnic, cinquefoil, chickweed, brittle fern and mullein. Climb grad-

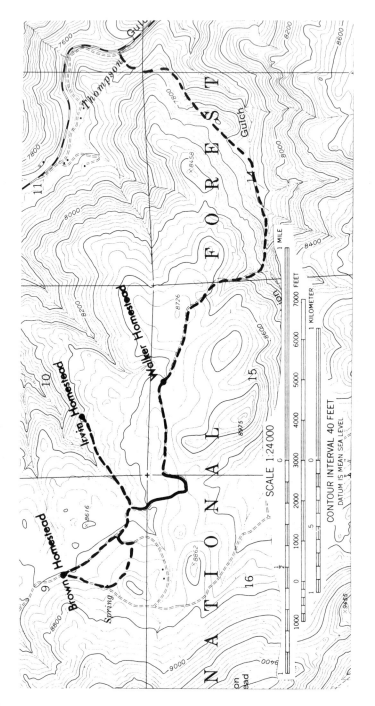

SCALE 1:24 000

CONTOUR INTERVAL 40 FEET
DATUM IS MEAN SEA LEVEL

156

ually and make another switchback. Pass several boulders and granitic outcroppings and drop downhill to pick up Lion Gulch. Walk below a cliff and cross the last bridge on the trail.

In the spring, purple fringe, buckwheat, parsley, sedges, snowberry, twisted star, false solomon seal, mountain ash and elderberry may be in bloom. The trail cuts uphill through a narrow canyon, crosses the stream several times and winds through moss covered spruce and fir. Walk through an open area with clumps of ponderosa pine and pick up an old road bed. Cross the stream over a culvert that appears to be the remains of an old boiler. Continue up the gulch to an open meadow and a trail junction. Stage Loop turns left, Sawmill Loop continues straight ahead to the Walker Homestead established in 1914.

The ruins represent four different types of log construction. The house, chicken coop and bunkhouse still stand. The open areas were used for growing potatoes and hay. The ranchers also logged the hillsides and sold the lumber in Meeker Park and Allenspark. Cattle roamed the meadows and hillside. Deer and elk were and are found in the area. Today camping is allowed but the forest service asks campers to camp away from the meadows, waterways and buildings to minimize human impact and to avoid disturbing the wildlife.

After leaving the Walker Homestead pick and follow a road that meanders up and down through a pine forest to the Meadow Loop, Sawmill Loop junction. A short walk along the Sawmill Loop leads to the Irvin Homestead, establihsed in 1917. Another Meadow Loop junction is passed on the way. The buildings at the Irvin site are in good repair. Several outbuildings including a chicken coop, wrangler cabin, bunkhouse and bathhouse circle the main house. The bathhouse has a "sunken bathtub" fed by gravity flow from a spring.

From the Irvin site a road continues to make a loop back to Lion Gulch, but the road ends and the trail that shows on the map has not been completed. It is a downhill trek to the gulch. Leave the old road at a rock outcropping and work cross-country down a gulch, being careful to stay away from the cliffs that border Lion Gulch. Come out about 100 yards above the stream boiler culvert.

It is possible to backtrack to the Meadow Loop, Sawmill

Irvin Homestead, 1917

Loop junction and pick up a road that leads to the Brown Homestead. The road winds through forests, open areas and hilly meadows to a large swampy meadow. Leave the road at the trail sign and walk to the remains of the Brown Homestead, established in 1919. Only one building remains at the site.

Follow the road south to a cairn to return to Sawmill Loop and pick up a trail near a rock cairn. The trail is faint in many places. Watch for cairns and climb uphill through a pine forest. Come out in a swampy meadow and follow the cairns to the edge of the swamp. Cross the end of the swamp, climb along a roadbed back to Sawmill Loop junction and return to Lion Gulch by way of the Walker Homestead.

The Sawmill Loop, Meadow Loop Trail system is on the Panora Peak Quadrangle. Other trails in the area that show on the map are hard to locate, and several trails are as yet to be completed. Either carry water or treat the water in the area because it is not safe to drink. Allow about six hours to hike and explore the area.

Elkhorn Creek

The unimproved trail along the lower section of Elkhorn Creek wanders through foothills-zone vegetation of juniper, narrowleaf cottonwood and alder with some rabbitbrush and mountain mahogany. The 4.5 mile hike, one way, has an elevation gain of 800 feet from its beginning at the Poudre River to the end at some picnic tables near the Manhattan Road cutoff from Log Cabin.

To reach the trailhead, drive 20.6 miles from Ted's Place at the entrance to the Poudre Canyon and cross the bridge over Elkhorn Creek at its junction with the Poudre River. Parking is available on the north side of Colorado 14.

Begin walking along a road and at the first junction stay to your right along the stream. The left branch climbs a steep hill and drops back to the stream.

Cross Elkhorn Creek and head into a narrow canyon with granitic rock exposed below sedimentary rock. Very shortly cross the stream a second time and continue walking along the hillside through Rocky Mountain juniper and a scattering of ponderosa pine and through a swampy grass area.

The trail winds by a dry knoll and twists below a jointed, eroded sentinel. Gradually bend west and then east as the stream makes a big 'S' curve around the base of a granite outcropping and push through willow, currant and alder. Climb above the stream, cross the stream and continue along the banks to another stream crossing.

A minor stream joins Elkhorn Creek from the northeast. Elkhorn bends gradually northwest to a crossing at an overhanging rock.

The canyon narrows and the stream is crossed near a large fallen ponderosa pine. Granite cliffs and outcroppings border each side of the stream. After crossing Elkhorn Creek again, walk through fallen ponderosa pine, standing juniper, spruce, fir, aspen and alder. Make two more crossings over the stream and hike through an open hillside. Come to a heavy stand of evergreens and cross the stream. Follow the canyon to an overhang and cross the stream. Pass through a fence, cross the

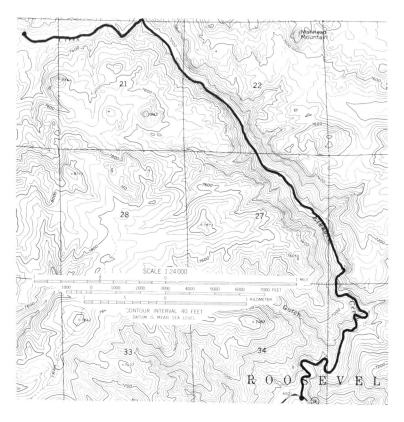

SCALE 1:24 000

1000   0   1000   2000   3000   4000   5000   6000   7000 FEET

1 MILE

1 KILOMETER

CONTOUR INTERVAL 40 FEET
DATUM IS MEAN SEA LEVEL

Elkhorn Creek Trail

stream, walk through more dead ponderosa pine and across a small drainage draw.

For a short distance the canyon opens. The trail cuts along the north side of the stream. Beautiful eroded outcroppings of granite border the trail. Before long the canyon narrows and can be hiked on either side of the stream. Pass through two fences in quick succession and pick up a jeep road as the canyon opens up. Walk to a road junction and turn right to reach the picnic tables.

Because there is so much bush hopping and stream crossing allow three hours one way to make the hike. In the spring, high water can cause problems, too, since there are no bridges along the way. Carry water or water purification tablets to treat the stream water which is not safe to drink.

Comanche Lake Trail

Comanche Lake is but one of several hikes that begin at Comanche Reservoir. The several trails are in good condition and fishing is reported to be good in the streams and lakes. During the summer months the area is heavily used but in early September through October, very few people are encountered. Black bear, deer, and elk reside in the area.

To reach the Reservoir and the trailhead, take Colorado 14 to the Pingree Park Road 25.7 miles from Ted's Place at the entrance to the Poudre Canyon. Turn onto the Pingree Park Road and continue 16.1 miles to the Tom Bennett Campground and turn right into the campground. Continue about 2.2 miles to the Sky Ranch property.

The road through the ranch could be closed but parking is permitted at the ranch. Begin a one mile hike that goes past the ranch buildings and to a trailhead located on the north side of the road. Hike two miles downhill through a stand of lodgepole and some spruce and pine. An old beaver pond can be seen filling in with sedges.

Comanche Lake

Both Hourglass Reservoir and Comanche Reservoir are seen from the trail. Walk along Beaver Creek and enter the Comanche Peak Wilderness just before reaching the reservoir. At the reservoir, take the trail that follows the north shore around it, making two downhill switchbacks over a boulder field. Walk along the level past a talus slope and into a burn area that occurred in 1966. After leaving the reservoir cross the bridge over Beaver Creek. Walk through the burn following the north side of the stream to a trail junction. Take the left hand branch to continue the one-mile hike to Comanche Lake. On the way, cross a stream and bend left. Make a switchback and zig-zag through the forest to another stream crossing and a trail junction. Turn right to reach the lake located in an oblong basin.

It is 6 miles one way with an elevation gain of 920 feet from the ranch. The trail from the ranch to the reservoir is a nice hike in itself and only 3 miles one way.

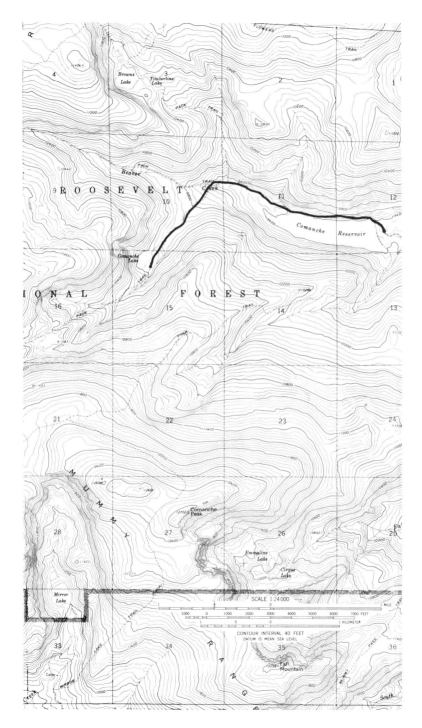

SCALE 1:24 000

CONTOUR INTERVAL 40 FEET
DATUM IS MEAN SEA LEVEL

Comanche Peak Trail

The 12,702 foot Comanche Peak in the Mummy Range is located near Comanche Reservoir on the boundary line of Rocky Mountain National Park. The trailhead is at Comanche Reservoir and can be reached by following the directions given under Comanche Lake Trail.

The peak, lake, and reservoir were named after Chief Comanche of the Ute Indians. He was known by some of the early settlers in the Cache La Poudre and Big Thompson Valleys. Comanche Peak is the steep-faced peak that rises to the northwest above the beautiful cirque lakes near Pingree Park in Roosevelt National Forest. The easiest route to the summit is from Comanche Reservoir. Follow the directions under Comanche Lake to reach the reservoir.

The hike begins at the face of the reservoir. Walk across the face of the dam in a southern direction and turn left towards a forest service outbuilding and an unnamed stream. At the stream the trail curves right to a mileage sign to Mirror Lake Trail and Mirror Lake. Begin a climb through a mature stand of trees next to the stream. Continue uphill along the stream to a steep pitch. Level out slightly and cross a spring. The trail winds at an erratic pace through the evergreens, downed timber and rocks and follows a long ridge. Climb through trees and open areas marked with cairns into alpine fir. Wind towards a large cirque with a permanent snowfield clinging to its face. Wind timber, gnarled, twisted clumps of spruce and fir crawl along the ground. When you reach the headwall of the huge snow-filled cirque you can pick out an unnamed peak and Comanche Peak.

Although the contour map shows a trail continuing to the high point west of the two peaks and then doubling back to the southwest, I have not been able to locate that trail. The one trail does continue over the flats in a western direction and eventually drops down to the Big South Fork of the Cache La Poudre River.

To reach Comanche Peak work around the top of the cirque through willow, hummock, seepage areas and ponds and head for the divide between the unnamed peak to the west and Comanche Peak in back and to the southeast of it. Climb over angular rocks and sandy debris interspersed between grassy areas to the saddle between the two peaks and head south to Comanche Peak.

As you walk through the tundra listen for the soft clucks and hoots of the white-tailed ptarmigan that reside in great numbers along the slopes leading to the peaks. The small birds are so well camouflaged that you are often only aware of their presence by their *kikiki* sounds.

The summit of Comanche is a pile of rocks stacked like a fallen pile of dominos. By walking a short distance to the south below the peak you can look down into the basin holding Emmaline and Cirque Lakes and some small tarns.

Southwest of Comanche Peak is the huge cirque that contains Mirror Lake. It is possible to continue to Mirror Lake by walking across the flats in a southwestern and then south direction to a steep downhill pitch that leads into the trees. Watch for cairns and pick them up for the route down. Come to the Mirror Lake junction, Corral Park junction. This trail is written up under Mirror Lake Trail, and, if you have someone to pick you up, you can continue to Corral Park.

It is approximately 8 miles to Comanche Peak from Comanche Reservoir with an elevation gain of 3,622 feet.

Comanche Peak

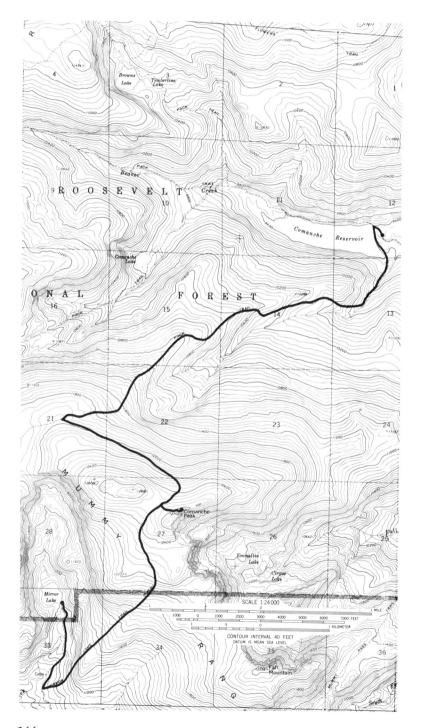

Long Draw Reservoir from Comanche Peak Trail

Comanche Reservoir to Browns Lake Trail

To reach the trailhead to Browns Lake from Comanche Reservoir follow the directions given for Comanche Lake. Begin hiking around the north shore of Comanche through the 1966 Comanche Burn that was caused by human carelessness and burned over 470 acres. Today lodgepole pine, aspen, wild raspberries and willow are filling in the burn. Come to a bridge crossing over a small stream and walk above the stream to a trail junction. Turn right, walk one-half mile to a second junction and turn right (north) for the final 1.5 mile hike to the lake. Climb uphill through the burn making 5 switchbacks to a long traverse that follows the contour of the stream to 2 more switchbacks.

Work in and out of the burn, past a granitic outcropping and gradually leave the burn. The trail levels temporarily before a slight climb past Timberline Lake just below Browns Lake. Cross the outlet stream on a bridge. It is 7.0 miles with 1,440 feet elevation gain to the lake.

Timberline Lake from trail to Browns Lake

Several variations are possible from Browns Lake. One is to continue to the Crown Point Road following the directions given under Browns Lake and have someone pick you up. Another variation is to continue uphill past a spring and cabin to a faint trail junction with a possible sign. Take off to the right (east) and follow the Old Flowers Road which is just a trail for 7 miles to Beaver Park written up under Beaver Park and then continue along the Beaver Park Trail to a needed car pick-up at the beginning of the Beaver Park Trail.

The trail to Beaver Park is faint in places but marked with cairns. For a time there is a slight uphill trek as you circle the base of Crown Point. There are excellent views of Comanche Peak and the Stormy Peaks along the way. Because the trail is used infrequently, it is an excellent place to see elk and deer.

After a climb over a small hump leave the tundra and drop into a spruce and fir forest. The forest composition changes as the trail drops downhill to an old roadbed. Follow the road to a bridge crossing over Little Beaver Creek and come to Beaver Park. Leave the wilderness area and walk along the Beaver Park road to a car pick-up. The total distance from Comanche Reservoir to Beaver Park is a good 11 miles with an additional 3.5 miles to a meeting point with a car. There is an elevation gain from Comanche Reservoir of 1,800 feet and a loss of 2,863 feet. There is no source of water after leaving the spring above Browns Lake until you reach Little Beaver Creek.

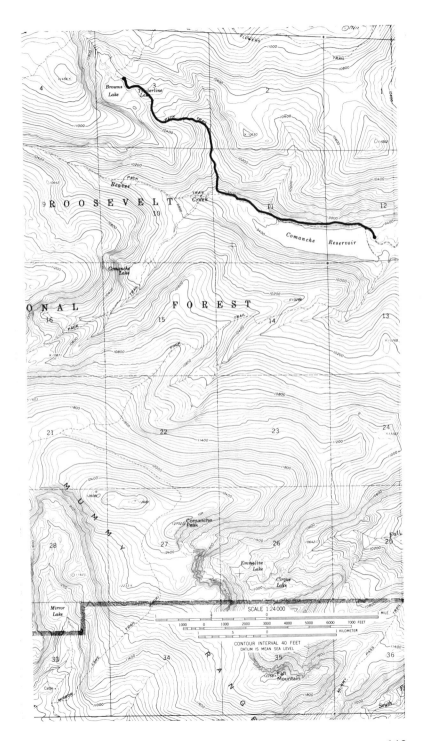

SCALE 1:24 000

CONTOUR INTERVAL 40 FEET
DATUM IS MEAN SEA LEVEL

169

Clark Peak viewed from unnamed peak to the northwest

Ruby Jewel Lake Trail

Jewel Lake looks more remote than it actually is. The beautiful tundra lake, named Ruby Jewel on the state forest service signs is at the base of 12,951 foot Clark Peak, the highest peak in the Rawah Wilderness. To reach the trailhead it is necessary to drive from Ted's Place at the entrance to the Poudre Canyon over Cameron Pass to the KOA Campground just past Gould at 75 miles. At the KOA Campground turn right onto a gravel road that leads to Michigan Reservoir. For a time the road is passable and well-marked with signs to Ruby Jewel and Kelly Lakes. However, the road becomes rough and nearly impossible for anything other than four-wheel drive vehicles. When it is no longer possible to drive, park and begin an approximate 2 mile hike through a pine forest along the road that leads to the trailhead which is near a sawmill pile and a trail sign.

From the sign, begin the remaining 1.5 mile hike by crossing a stream and making a turn to the left. Walk along the edge of a willow bottom with two unnamed peaks on each side of the trail. Begin a steady climb through subalpine fields of paintbrush, penstemon, climbing bell and larkspur. Come to a stream and follow it to a crossing.

Cross a meadow, walk by a slash pile and continue along the edge of a willow bottom. To the right of the trail is a beautiful waterfall. At a split in the trail, take the higher trail which is a new trail and climb to a talus slope with a rock formation on the summit that resembles a javelin. Make two switchbacks, cross the talus, round a point and head toward the talus slopes of Clark Peak and an unnamed peak. The trail winds through a swampy meadow below a bench like talus. Marsh-marigold, queens crown, kings crown, yellow paintbrush, solomonseal and daisies fill the meadow with color.

From the meadow, the trail can be seen winding up to the saddle of Clark Peak but this is not the best way to climb the peak. Once the trail reaches the saddle, it is an up and down climb before ever reaching the summit. It is easier to climb the peak from the northeast end of Ruby Jewel Lake.

Ruby Jewel Lake

To continue to the lake, cross the outlet stream from Ruby Jewel and walk east over an alpine slope. Bend north and climb toward some rock outcroppings and over the west or left knoll to the lake.

A few scraggly trees rim the south end of the lake. To the north is an unnamed peak of 12,654 feet and to the northeast is 12,951 foot Clark Peak.

To climb the peak walk to the north end of the lake and begin a steep, slow scramble up loose rock to the saddle between the two peaks. At the saddle turn right and continue a steep scramble to the summit. From the summit, the Branch Lakes and Blue Lake can be seen to the east and northeast. To the west is North Park.

Allow four hours to reach the lake and the summit of Clark Peak. There is an elevation gain of 1,200 feet to the lake from the trailhead and 2,911 feet to the summit of Clark Peak.

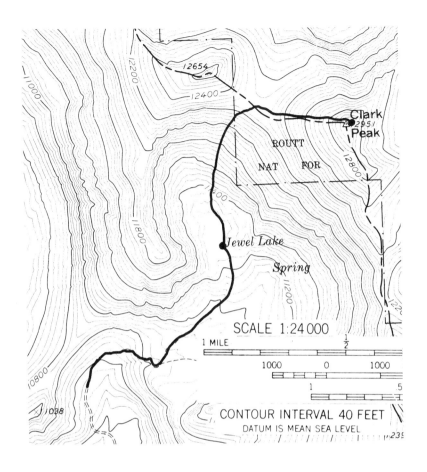

SCALE 1:24 000

1 MILE

1000   0   1000

1

CONTOUR INTERVAL 40 FEET
DATUM IS MEAN SEA LEVEL

Clark
Peak

ROUTT

NAT   FOR

Jewel Lake

Spring

Lost Lake and Rawah Lakes Trail

The hike to the Rawah Lakes from the Rawah Ranch is 10 miles, almost too far for a one day hike, but Lost Lake, 7 miles from the trailhead, makes a nice one day hike. The pear-shaped lake is off the main trail one-half mile and is surrounded by a panoply of evergreens and a rock cliff to the southwest.

To reach the trailhead follow the directions under Branch Lakes to the Woods Landing Road. Turn north at the junction and drive 11.8 miles to the trailhead near the Rawah Ranch.

The first part of the trail cuts through private property along a forest access. The Laramie River is crossed and after a level walk through swamp and willow, you leave private property and enter Roosevelt National Forest. Continue along the level through lodgepole to an upgrade in the trail and bend through aspen and pine to four switchbacks. The trail continues through the forest to a switchback and follows Rawah Creek to a bridge crossing. Make one switchback after crossing the stream and follow it to a waterfall and another switchback. Climb over a low foot of a knoll and trek through aspen to a switchback and overlook of the Laramie River.

Resume climbing for a time to a level area that winds through boulders, open areas, aspen and pine and climb over two switchbacks to a small stream which is crossed. Very shortly climb up ten switchbacks. The forest gradually changes to a mixture of spruce, fir and pine with a jumbled understory of down timber, small trees and huckleberry. Near the last switchback, the trail winds around a knobby tree covered granite mound. The trail continues uphill past boulders to four more switchbacks that lead to the top side of the mound. It is then downhill through a heavy stand of evergreens. Cross a stream and come to a forest service sign. The trail switchbacks out of the stream drainage and, after a short hike, enters the Rawah Wilderness. Continue along the level, gradually working uphill. Cross a stream and immediately come to a trail junction at the northeast end of the Rawah Bog which is below the trail. The trail to the right (north) leads to Lost Lake. There may or may not be a sign.

Lost Lake

The section of the trail to Lost Lake is unimproved. It zig-zags steeply uphill to two minor switchbacks and then a third one to the top of a ridge. Level out and walk around a swamp and a small pool that is to the right of you and very quickly pass two more small ponds. Wind through the trees and drop downhill 165 feet to Lost Lake.

Allow four hours to make the seven mile hike with an elevation gain of 1,775 feet.

To continue to the Rawah Lakes, walk around the Rawah Bog. At the wide part of the Bog bend south and then climb. Come to a stream crossing and level out as you walk along the stream to a trail junction. Stay to your right (west). The left junction leads to the Sandbar Lakes and Big Rainbow Lake. Follow a meadow and come to McIntyre-Link Trail junction. Turn left (south) and very shortly come to No. 1 of the Rawah Lakes. There is an elevation gain of 2,160 feet in the ten mile hike to the first of the Rawah Lakes.

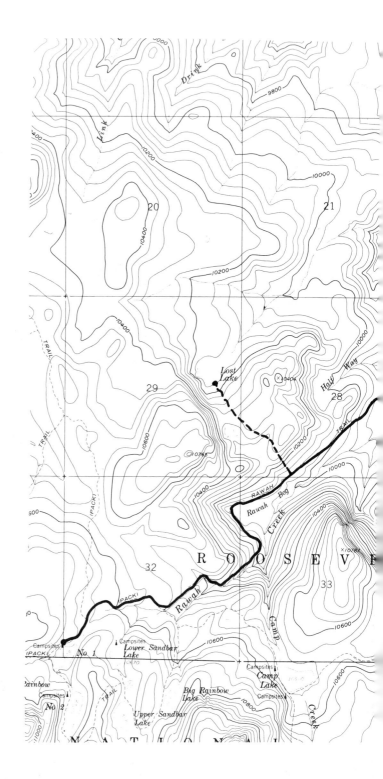

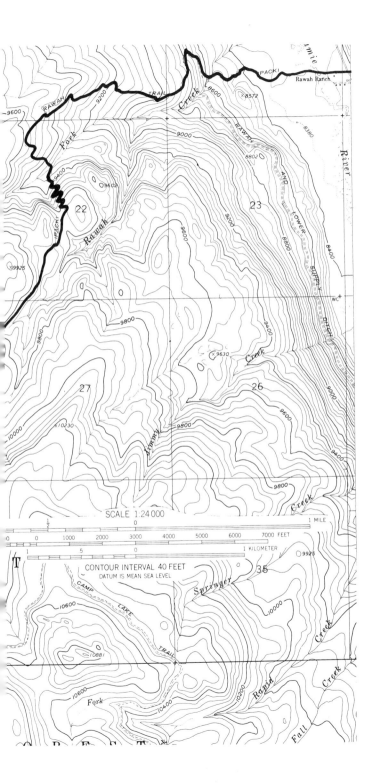

SCALE 1:24 000

CONTOUR INTERVAL 40 FEET
DATUM IS MEAN SEA LEVEL

Index